# minds
## in
# motion

## using museums
## to expand
## creative thinking

### alan gartenhaus

### expanded third edition

# minds in *motion*
## using museums
## to expand creative thinking

By Alan R. Gartenhaus

Third Edition 1997 (Revised and Expanded)
Second Edition 1993
First Edition 1991
Copyright 1991, 1993, and 1997 by Alan Gartenhaus

Published by Caddo Gap Press
   3145 Geary Boulevard, Suite 275
   San Francisco, California 94118 U.S.A.
E-mail caddogap@aol.com

Price: $14.95

ISBN: 1-880192-21-7

Library of Congress Cataloging-in-Publication Data

Gartenhaus, Alan Reid.
  Minds in motion : using museums to expand creative thinking   Alan
Gartenhaus. -- Expanded 3rd ed.
    p.   cm.
  Includes bibliographical references.
  ISBN 1-880192-21-7 (alk. paper)
  1. Museums--Educational aspects.   2. Creative thinking.
3. Museums--United States--Directories.   I. Title.
AM7.G34  1997
069'.15--dc21                                          96-30100
                                        CIP

# Table of Contents

# Dedication

This book is dedicated to the memory of Shirley Gartenhaus, my Mother, who stimulated my interest in museums and education, and who insisted I learn how to type.

## Acknowledgements

A number of people contributed to the making of this book. They include: J. Littleton, who provided invaluable editorial assistance and encouragement; the trustees and staff of the Northwood Institute's Creativity Center, for the Fellowship that got me started; and R. Lee, for reasons too numerous to mention.

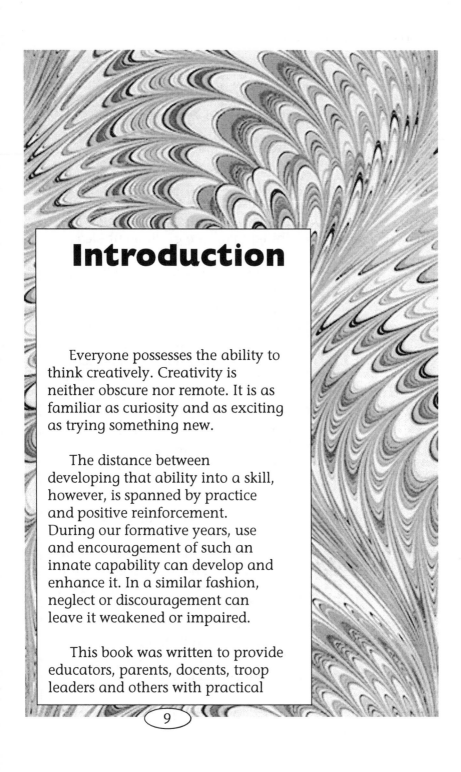

# Introduction

Everyone possesses the ability to think creatively. Creativity is neither obscure nor remote. It is as familiar as curiosity and as exciting as trying something new.

The distance between developing that ability into a skill, however, is spanned by practice and positive reinforcement. During our formative years, use and encouragement of such an innate capability can develop and enhance it. In a similar fashion, neglect or discouragement can leave it weakened or impaired.

This book was written to provide educators, parents, docents, troop leaders and others with practical methods for exercising and reinforcing creative thinking among children and young adults. These activities are not age restrictive, however, and can also be used and enjoyed by adults. The goal is the same for all — to establish productive opportunities for using the imagination and for thinking of new or different ideas.

What makes this text different from others of its kind is that it takes advantage of a most exceptional setting — the museum. Museum collections contain authentic and fascinating objects, providing excellent tools to engage the mind and set it into motion. Although word games or puzzles can be interesting, museum objects are mentally stimulating, inherently important, and often, visually exciting.

Consider this — You are walking through a history museum. You turn a corner, and there before you is an old backpack. You read that it was carried by a fifteen-year-old Civil War soldier who died at the Battle of Bull Run. What might he have carried in that pack? Was there some small reminder of the home and family he left behind? Feel the weight of that pack on your back as you march with him to fight against his cousins in Virginia. What thoughts are going through your mind?

Now imagine yourself in the gallery of an art museum. You stand before a bizarre and distorted portrait. The figure is grotesque. Even the paint seems to have been alternately thrown against, or gouged from, the canvas. What response does this portrait evoke in you? What details or specific aspects of the painting make you feel this way? How many other ways might the artist have conveyed the same emotions?

Or, you are in a natural history museum. You come upon the fossilized footprint of a Diplodocus, a prehistoric creature. How is the footprint similar to others you have seen? In what ways is it different? How many things can be told about this massive lifeform just by examining its footprint?

Museum collections ignite the imagination. They are a rich resource for diverse experiences because of the many stories they tell, the varieties of information they convey, and the different ideas they suggest. While any object could be used to enhance creative thinking, museum objects are among the highest caliber of stimuli.

# Creative Thinking

## What is creativity?

Creativity is not a mystery, though its definition is elusive. Creativity is familiar; it is known to each of us because we have experienced it. Few of us, however, have been encouraged to develop and strengthen it.

During the formative years spent in school, children are taught to think of "correct responses." Historical dates, rules for punctuation, and multiplication tables are memorized and tested.

Such convergent thought processes as memorization and literal comprehension become familiar and well-practiced skills.

## "Convergent" vs. "divergent" thinking

While the developing minds of young people are trained to think *convergently*, their *divergent* thinking abilities are often neglected. Convergent thinking focuses, or "converges," thoughts in order to determine correct answers. Divergent thinking permits thoughts to expand, or "diverge," in order to encompass many possible solutions to questions having many objective right answers, or perhaps none at all.

Divergent thinking is useful for responding to the majority of life's complex questions, which tend to be open-ended. They challenge people to consider a range of possibilities, alternatives and consequences. These questions have no fixed answers. They call upon divergent thinking and individual perspective. They invite myriad possible responses. They are unlike most academic questions encountered in school.

"Should I go to college?"
"What do I do with my spare time?"
"What kind of job do I want?"
Finding the most appropriate
answers to such questions first
requires generating a range of
possibilities, alternatives, and
outcomes. Only then, after
comparing possibilities against
others, can the wisest choices be
made.

Creativity's source is divergent
thinking. It is how new ideas are
developed, and how possibilities,
alternatives, and options are
generated.

Until they reach school age,
children's divergent thinking is
likely to be rewarded. Youngsters
"make-believe." They constantly
ask "why" and "why not,"
challenging the assumptions of the
adult world. These precocious
behaviors earn praise. When the
schooling and socialization
processes begin, however,
imagination and invention are
often discouraged in favor of being
practical, predictable, and correct.
It is at this early stage that
convergent thinking begins to
dominate.

Ironically, as young people approach adulthood, with minds well practiced at convergent thinking, more of life's divergent, or open-ended, questions present themselves. To manage the uncertainty and anxiety that result from this contradiction and imbalance, at least two response mechanisms are developed: habit and opinion. Each leads back to the comfort zone of having a "right" answer.

Habit and opinion make open-ended problems seem far less intimidating. It is much easier to fall back upon previously formed responses and patterns than it is to consider the many variables and opportunities presented by new situations.

Assuming that all successful people go to college; routinely watching television regardless of programming; or accepting the notion that one should go into the family business regardless of their other interests or talents, are examples of habitual or prejudicial thinking. Each is a response developed without considering alternatives. Though they relieve us of the responsibilities and insecurities associated with uncertainty, they may not be the most satisfactory responses to a changing and challenging world.

So, in addition to skilled divergent thinking, creativity avoids habit, routine, and prejudice in the quest for improvement, change, and personal growth. Creativity is a useful "tool" that can make things happen or that can develop new states of awareness.

Perhaps for our purposes this information is enough to develop an acceptable elementary, working definition of creativity.

It has been determined that creativity has several components:

1: divergent thinking;

2: open-mindedness to new ways of thinking regardless of what one is predisposed to believe; and

3: an aim toward new understandings and change.

It can be said, then, that "creativity is an ability to generate ideas and possibilities, beyond the functions of habit and opinion, which lead to personal discovery, change, and a higher level of understanding."

## Shouldn't an idea be unique to be considered creative?

"Uniqueness" is a complex issue. Creativity is often associated with the unique, the one-of-a-kind. Artists are assumed to be creative because their works actually are one-of-a-kind, and tangible evidence of individuality. Scientists are thought to be creative when they are the first, if not the only, person to discover a major principle, invention, or cure.

Creativity is not a product, however. What is seen when viewing art, examining scientific discoveries, or marveling at new mechanical devices are the end products of creative thinking. Creativity is a thought process and not a "thing."

Creativity can remain intangible. It need not, and most often does not, result in some "thing." As Edward de Bono, founder of the Center for the Study of Thinking and Cognitive Research Trust at Cambridge University, defines it, "Creative thinking includes personal processes, such as new ways of looking at things, new ways of organizing things, and new attitudes or new ideas about ideas."

People are creative when they discover, reorder, or think of something that is new to them. It does not matter whether others thought of the same possibility or idea before. Creative thinking occurs on a personal level. Questions of "first" or "only" are not relevant. A creative thought is one that is unique or new to the person thinking it.

## People have to be really smart to be creative, don't they?

Most of us have heard stories of brilliant people who did poorly in school, or who were even asked to leave. Thomas Edison was one. His teachers considered him to be "addled." He was diagnosed as a "slow and disinterested learner."

Albert Einstein was another; he failed mathematics. Perhaps creative thinking does not always fit into narrow, school-specific definitions of "smart?"

Even the idea of "smart" seems relative. Who is smart? When are we smart? A teenager who gets straight "A's" on his report card is considered smart. But, if that same teenager gets in trouble for reckless driving we tell him, "that wasn't very smart, was it?"

Whether a person is smart or not has everything to do with the context or situation. Being "street smart" is very different than being "book smart." Being smart verbally is very different than being smart mathematically. Intelligence, like most things in life, just does not fit into neat little categories. Ambiguities are certain to arise when trying to quantify or qualify "smart."

If we agree, for the moment, that being smart has something to do with exceptional functioning of the brain, then we find that there are actually several manifestations of "smart." They include, but are not limited to:

**general intellectual**: the talent to understand and learn with ease, use logic, and remember well;

**specific academic**: the aptitude to excel in a single subject, such as chemistry, while remaining average in most everything else;

**leadership**: the facility to inspire, shape, or speak on behalf of, public opinion;

**artistically gifted**: the ability to translate thought and emotion through painting, dancing, music, or another art form;

**psychomotor**: the talent needed to become an exceptional athlete; and

**creative**: the ability to generate original or inventive thoughts, and/or the ability to find new insights, relationships, and worthwhile imaginings.

Perhaps you can think of other types of "smart."

Without a doubt, it is helpful to have a solid intellectual foundation, but this by itself does not qualify someone as creative.

Conversely, one can be very creative without having exceptional intellectual functions or an outstanding academic record. Being smart is not a determining factor for creativity; creativity is just one of many ways of being smart.

## If there are types of "smart," are there types of "creative?"

Education authorities E. Paul Torrance and J.P. Guilford have observed that creative thinkers generate their thoughts and ideas in at least four main ways. These four processes are not the only ways to be creative; however, they do represent convenient categories to use when attempting to understand creative thinking patterns. Each of these attributes may exist independently of the others, or in combination.

**1: Fluency.** Fluent thinking is the facility for producing a *quantity* of possibilities, ideas, or consequences. Fluent thinkers generate a disproportionately large number of ideas. Fluent thinkers often have "just one more thing" to add, long after a discussion seems to be exhausted.

**2: Flexibility.** Flexible thinking is the ability to develop a *variety* of perspectives. Flexible thinkers perform a kind of mental gymnastics as they seek several ways to approach a single problem. Flexible thinkers may challenge authority because they see alternatives to the "one way" of doing something.

**3: Originality.** Original thinking is the ability to produce unusual, unique, or highly *personalized* responses or ideas. Original thinkers, and their novel responses, may be considered eccentric or just plain peculiar. Original thinkers often delight, or confound, their teachers, parents, or peers by the manner in which they solve tasks and problems.

**4: Elaboration.** Elaborative thinking is the ability to expand, develop, and *embellish* ideas. Elaborative thinkers are fascinated by, and with, details. They seem to notice more than other people, or give greater attention to "texture" and "richness" in what they do. Elaborative thinkers are often drawn to the complex and the complicated.

Perhaps you have already identified these characteristics in a child, or yourself. Perhaps you've observed behavior that now can be understood as evidence of creativity. This is not uncommon. Since all of us have inherent creative potential, these traits do remain in evidence. They are most evident in the overt behavior of young children, however, because they have not yet learned to suppress their innate creative abilities.

## If everyone is born a creative thinker, why aren't most of us better at it?

Most children are tested to determine their "I.Q.," or intelligence quotient. I.Q. tests do not measure the amount of knowledge possessed, since a child's level of knowledge is comparatively low. Intelligence tests are meant to quantify a person's potential to acquire knowledge and think logically.

If children were also tested for

their creativity quotient, or "C.Q.," it would be found that each has a particular potential for generating ideas, thoughts and imaginings. This score would quantify their potential to think in an expansive and divergent manner.

Throughout the formal education processes, thinking abilities measured by intelligence tests are exercised and practiced, while those that reinforce creative thinking are often neglected or actually inhibited. This results in an imbalance between these two complementary thinking skills.

The imbalance can be likened to a weightlifter who only exercised the left side of his body. While the left side would grow stronger and more powerful, the right would become weaker and more dependent. Regardless of how he tried to compensate, his overall strength would be diminished. Only with both sides exercised and strong would he achieve balance and be able to realize his full potential.

But thinking isn't lifting weights. People don't purposefully exercise some aspects of their thinking abilities and abandon others. What prevents people from better actualizing their creativity quotient? Why doesn't it continue to develop and strengthen over time?

For some, creative thinking seems to flourish in spite of obstacles. For most, however, school, society and speed may be among the main culprits squelching creativity. Each works in its own way to discourage individual perspective and the practice of creative thinking.

The lessons and examinations of school teach young people to memorize "right" answers. Consistent with the break-up of subjects into limited periods of time, students also come to view subjects as disconnected from one another. Pressures created by the teacher's grade book, parental expectations, and the evaluation of peers can heighten the fear of failure, end risk-taking, and reduce individuality through pressure to conform.

Everyday experiences in contemporary society can further the imbalance. Visual images and messages bombard us on everything from billboards to cereal boxes. Sound recordings bring orchestras and rock groups into homes, cars, and on walks through forests. Television's constant potential to entertain is ever-present. All this makes using our imaginations and inventiveness far less necessary and lessens the time spent in quiet reflection.

Ours is the "fast age," where a primary objective is the pursuit of speed, or instant gratification. "Good" is measured less by quality than by rapidity. Today, we value fast food, fast relief from pain, and fast answers. Abbreviated presentation of the news on television appears to simplify problems and decrease the need to read, seek out facts, and analyze meanings and consequences. Convenience items such as cameras that focus and set exposures automatically, or calculators that add and subtract for us, speed up these processes, bypassing learning and problem-solving. They teach us that we need not learn from our mistakes. Indeed, we need not make attempts, much less mistakes.

This discourse is not meant to be an indictment of our schools, our

society, or our quest for speed.
Each has evolved in response to
needs and desires. No technology is
inherently bad, either. Indeed,
among other reasons, many were
developed to handle convergent
thinking activities so that we might
be free to think more divergently.
Nonetheless, all of these forces mold
our behaviors and effect thinking
patterns. Their cumulative effects
are powerful shapers of our
attention, concentration,
imagination, and problem-solving
skills.

## Should we want children to be more creative?

There is an old adage that states,
"Nothing succeeds like success."
With each victory or success comes
the courage and self-confidence to
try again and move ahead.
As a child learns to ride a two-wheel
bike she may at first be hesitant.
After several attempts, however,
she begins to believe in her ability
to do it. Suddenly, that child is up
and riding and the mechanics of
riding are no longer an issue.
Now, riding is a skill, and the bike a
"tool" for getting from place to

place rather than an obstacle to be conquered.

Confidence in one's creativity can grow from each creative thinking experience. When young people find themselves making real advances — generating new ideas and gaining new insights from their ideas — it reinforces their desire to achieve further. Ultimately, their abilities will strengthen because they will want them to.

An improved self-concept can be another reward. If a child views himself as uncreative and dependent upon the wisdom, advice, ideas or products of others, his self-concept will lower and sense of dependency increase. He may eventually discount his own abilities, believing he can only learn or understand from the insights and expertise of others. Reinforcing and exercising creative thinking strengthens faith in one's own capabilities, and allows the views and ideas developed by others to be placed in context.

With increased motivation and a strengthened concept of self, young people will want to, and believe themselves capable of, learning and growing. They will begin to appreciate and trust their own abilities to discover or uncover concepts and ideas. They will gain a healthy mental independence by learning a measure of mental self-reliance.

## Can creativity actually be learned?

Creativity is not simply a matter of divine inspiration, nor is it special insight that the fortunate few will receive by a stroke of good fortune. Creative thinking is a skill. The research of countless authorities, including Alex Osborn, Sidney Parnes, Angelo Biondi, and Donald Treffinger, to name only a few, conclude that creativity can be provoked and, with practice, increased.

Developing greater facility for fluency, flexibility, originality and elaboration exercise creative thinking at its most essential level — the production of divergent thoughts. It also provides a model for circumventing habitual or prejudicial response patterns.

As young people become more

practiced at divergent thinking, they will gain a sense of independence and confidence that will remain with them through each new situation or problem. They will have the opportunity to develop a fuller range of thinking abilities.

The three "S's" (school, society, and speed) teach of the importance of information, the need to work quickly, and the knowledge that one must fulfill the expectations of others. These are important lessons. However, training in creative thinking provides a balance. It demonstrates how much can be learned by making attempts, regardless of outcomes. It introduces the virtues of taking time and the delights that may be found within the tiniest details. It offers routes for the expression of individual differences and an appreciation for differing perspectives. Practice in creative thinking can reveal the rewards to be found in being one's self.

By teaching children how they can draw upon their own unique resources, you provide them with the tools they need to continually learn, grow, and become more effective thinkers and problem-solvers.

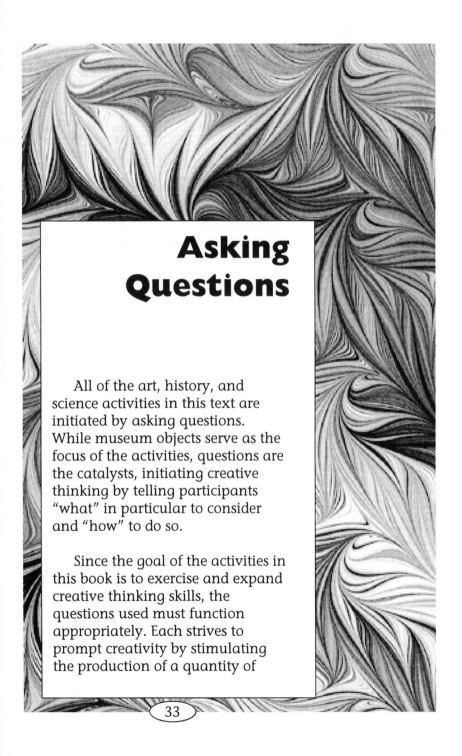

# Asking Questions

All of the art, history, and science activities in this text are initiated by asking questions. While museum objects serve as the focus of the activities, questions are the catalysts, initiating creative thinking by telling participants "what" in particular to consider and "how" to do so.

Since the goal of the activities in this book is to exercise and expand creative thinking skills, the questions used must function appropriately. Each strives to prompt creativity by stimulating the production of a quantity of ideas (fluency), or a wide variety of ideas (flexibility), or highly personalized ideas (originality), or highly embellished ideas (elaboration).

## What questions provoke creative thinking best?

Not all questions jump-start creativity. In fact, some do just the opposite. Questions that test a person's recall of specific information, such as "What year did the first settlers arrive at Jamestown, Virginia?" or that challenge a person's perceptual abilities, such as "How many trees do you see in this landscape painting?" are designed to evoke a specific, correct response.

Questions that have correct or predetermined answers are closed-ended. While such questions are useful for testing whether facts or abilities have been learned or remembered, they neither request, nor accommodate, creativity. Open-ended questions, on the other hand, are questions that do not have presupposed or predetermined answers. They embrace a wide variety of responses, and call upon our individual creativity to formulate a range of possibilities.

For instance, the question, "What is the distance in miles between Jacksonville, Florida, and Los Angeles, California, if driving on Interstate 10?" is closed-ended. It is not subject to interpretation. There is a specific, correct answer. However, the question "How many different ways might you measure the distance between Jacksonville, Florida, and Los Angeles, California?" is open-ended. This question has many possible responses, including:

- by miles;
- by kilometers;
- by the time it takes to drive at different speeds;
- by the number of steps it takes to walk;
- by the calories it burns to walk;
- by the time it takes to fly on different types of aircraft;
- by fuel consumption using different types of transportation;
- by the number of geo-political units (states or counties) you would pass through;

- by the time zones you would pass through;
- by how far away the cities "feel" when a loved one is in the other location;
- by the cost of a bus, train, or plane ticket;
- by the amount of string it would take to span between the two cities; and so forth.

## How do open-ended questions work?

Just as there are two types of thinking — convergent and divergent — there are two types of questions — closed-ended and open-ended. Closed-ended questions request convergent thinking, challenging the mind to narrow its focus to a specific answer, or specific set of answers. Open-ended questions call for the production of ideas, thoughts, and imaginings. They invite the mind to think divergently, acting as a pry to open thinking up in order to generate new, different, or more possibilities.

Open-ended questions call for the "creation" of possibilities because they ask for them. In other words, open-ended questions prompt fluent, flexible, original, or elaborative thinking by their construction. For instance:

- questions or tasks designed to provoke a greater quantity of responses often incorporate phrases like, "How many...can you think of?" or "Develop a list of as many...as you possibly can." Such interrogatives request fluent thinking.

- questions or tasks that serve to provoke a greater variety of responses often begin with phrases such as, "How else might you consider...?" or "What other kind of answer can you think of...?" These interrogatives invite flexible thinking.

- questions or tasks that provoke highly personalized responses should specifically request this form of thinking from participants. Phrases such as, "What would **you** do...?" or "Come up with **your very own**...." can prompt original thinking by challenging participants to develop individualized ideas.

- questions or tasks that provoke highly detailed responses might begin with such phrases as, "Tell us more about...." or "What else do you know about ...?" Such interrogatives extract detailed or additional information from participants through elaborative thinking.

## What kinds of responses are offered to open-ended questions?

"Ask an open-ended question, get a multitude of responses." Because they are designed to encourage the production of options more than answers, open-ended questions will elicit responses ranging from the predictable to the hardly credible. Some will seem clever; others will seem "off-the-wall." Keep in mind, however, that the reason for asking these questions is to have young people practice creative thinking, and NOT to have them come up with or retrieve correct answers.

Remember that the responses you receive will reflect differences in individual points-of-view. All participants will see, think about, and decide different things when inspecting museum objects. Even when they are looking at the very same object, people will selectively focus and respond in their own, personalized way.

## How should I react to the range of responses received?

Creative thinking can be encouraged or discouraged simply by the manner in which you, as the group leader, react. Participation and the communication of ideas are based on trust — trust that one's thoughts will be valued and that one's attempts will be positively recognized. If anyone has an inkling that his or her thoughts are not respected, that person may quit participating, withdraw, and even shut down creative thought all-together.

Your responsibility when leading

activities such as these is to facilitate and encourage creative thinking and participation, NOT to sit in judgment. Be open to new, wild, humorous, or highly idiosyncratic thoughts. If you, or others in the group, are highly puzzled by a response, request elaboration. Without seeming to challenge the respondent, ask for more information or to understand how the person decided upon a particular idea. Then, accept the reasoning offered and move on.

Sometimes, participants will offer answers that they, themselves, will re-evaluate after more ideas are put forth or with additional time for reflection. That's fine. But as the facilitator, you should be encouraging production and not evaluation. These exercises are the equivalent of "brainstorming" sessions. Their purpose is the creation of possibilities, not the critiquing answers.

Though it will be difficult, avoid employing positive judgments to reward or encourage responses that you like. Young people quickly learn the difference between being told, "good answer" and being told "okay." The lack of a positive reaction is the equivalent of a negative reaction to most people. Remain consistent in both the type and the tone of your reactions.

Remember that everyone seeks validation from a group leader. Try to avoid having participants work for your approval, rather than for the internal satisfaction of thinking creatively. Offer such non-judgmental statements as "thank you" when acknowledging responses from participants.

Use your own open-ended questions to encourage additional fluent, flexible, original, or elaborative thinking. Ask participants if they can come up with another thought, or a different way of thinking about something.

Be patient. Do not expect responses immediately after asking a question or establishing a task. Give participants time to think, reflect, and reconsider. It takes time to think creatively.

## Notes

# Using Museums

Museums come in many varieties, sizes, and forms, but each presents a full range of subjects and ideas to consider. In museums, we can be sent on journeys to faraway lands, to earlier times, or to worlds found through the microscope.

Whether presenting the familiar or exotic, the personal or universal, museums can be used to stimulate the imagination and provoke creativity.

Creativity is fostered best when young people are interested and enthusiastic about the subject matter. Museum exhibitions can be used to encourage the expression of individual interests because they present objects that can be understood and appreciated from a variety of disciplines and points of view. Natural history specimens might be appreciated for their aesthetic qualities. Works of art can be enjoyed for their historical significance. Objects from earlier times might be considered in light of their economic impact.

The exhibit halls of museums are open spaces, and the objects they contain can often be viewed in random fashion. Even in museums with directional exhibitions, young people are free to focus their attention in response to what "catches their eye," without regard to predetermined order or instructions. Museums allow us to wander among objects the way thoughts might wander among ideas.

Thus, museums provide excellent provocation to creativity because they present interesting objects, imbued with great significance, which can be approached from a variety of directions, both mentally and physically. Museums can put minds into motion without pre-determining their destination.

Museums offer many services to the general public, including tours of their collections. Though most do not require tours for groups of young people, they often request adult chaperones. Should you be leading more than several children through the museum, using the activities in this book, you may wish to contact the museum before arriving to inform them.
Few museum tours are designed specifically to provoke creative thinking. Therefore, if a tour is taken,  it will work better if it follows the activities you conduct.

## Which museum should be used?

There are many kinds of museums. Some museums have general areas of interest, such as museums of natural history or larger museums of art.
Other museums restrict their collections to a single, very specific area such as clocks, or automobiles, or African art. There are even museums designed for specific

audiences, like "children's museums."

There are museums that are not even called museums. Historic homes, interpretive parks, nature centers, and zoos can all be considered types of museums since they maintain and exhibit collections for educational purposes.

No matter where you live, there are likely to be several museums within close proximity to your home. (For information about museums in your area, or while traveling, see the list of museums at the back of this book.) If you have a choice, select a museum by the subject area that interests you and your children most. Regardless of which museum you use, the objects they contain can stimulate creative thinking abilities.

# Does it take great knowledge to use a museum well?

Using museums to promote creative thinking differs from using museums to learn "art history" or "the laws of natural science." The goal is to exercise a thought process, not to gain specific information.

Conducting the exercises in this book does not require or assume an informational background. Questions that arise from creative thinking exercises may take you beyond what you know, regardless of how much or how little information you have. Should this occur, or should you prefer not to provide answers to factual questions, you might suggest researching the answers as a productive follow-up to the museum visit.

Who we are, what we have experienced, and what interests us determines where our imaginations take us. Having little "academic" knowledge of subject matter is not a barrier to the imagination. In fact the reverse may be true. Knowledge can sometimes prevent us from conjecturing, by pinning us down to predetermined notions.

## How should the museum be used to promote creativity?

Working on your creative thinking skills in a museum is easy. Ideas tend to build upon one another. The objects children encounter in a museum will be used to provide them with "first ideas." These objects serve as springboards, or points of departure, for their own additional ideas, alternatives, and insights.

The following are suggestions that will assist you when conducting children through a museum to exercise their creativity:

**1: Focus on objects that capture attention and interest.** Do not select objects because they are deemed most important or because of recognizable names or dates. Unless specifically instructed to do otherwise, select objects that naturally tend to intrigue. For purposes of stimulating creative thinking, these will work best.

**2: Do not feel that children must be exposed to everything in the museum.** Regardless of size, museums can be overwhelming if you try to see everything. Allow objects to capture attention.
Should you wish to see more than you have time for while working on creativity, plan a return visit.
If you are far from home or on a field trip, and should you feel compelled to see it all on this one visit, take a brisk tour through the rest of the museum after working with several objects in-depth.

**3: Children can work alone or with others.** While it is perfectly appropriate to work alone, it is sometimes more fun to work with others. Creative thinkers do borrow and build upon shared ideas.
In fact, should children feel stumped, it is advisable to have them get ideas from each other. Often, these ideas will stimulate more of their own. If you are working with one child, participate in the activity together.

**4: Take time; do not rush.**
The artist Georgia O'Keefe said, "To see takes time, like to have a friend takes time." Stay and explore an object fully, pushing creative

and perceptual abilities to the limit, before moving on. The first several ideas people have are already in mind. These are perhaps our least creative thoughts. Exercising creativity comes when we strain to think of something else. It is natural and appropriate that it take time for momentum to build.

**5: Avoid reading labels first.** Labeling something, even with objective information, begins to define it. For purposes of exercising creativity, focus children's attention on what interests them about an object, rather than what the museum tells about it. After they have challenged themselves creatively, they are free to read labels and any other information they choose.

**6: Encourage children to take mental risks.** Do not inhibit, or allow others to inhibit, thoughts simply because they seem foolish, wild, or silly. Sometimes these thoughts turn out to be very productive. Consider the "wild" idea that man could fly and the invention of aircraft. Remember, creative thinking is expansive and allows for all thoughts. The emphasis is on *having* ideas, not judging them.

**7: Making collective judgments about objects should be suspended.** When judgments like "it is not very good" are made together, open-minded consideration on an individual level often ends. Even positive judgments can define or narrow how something is perceived.
Unless otherwise instructed for the purposes of an activity, try to shift attention and conversation away from value judgments and decisions until after possibilities and alternatives have been explored.

**8: Take even more time!**
The purpose of the activities in this book is to stimulate and exercise creative thinking abilities.
As with any form of exercise, "no pain, no gain." Continue to seek more ideas after it is no longer easy. This is how creative abilities are worked and strengthened.

NOTE: When working on exercises that require writing, use pencils. Most museums do not permit the use of pens in exhibit halls and galleries. Also, use small notebooks for writing. They will be less cumbersome than using pieces of paper, and they provide their own surface to write on. Never allow anyone to touch, or write upon, objects or the object cases. The museum's first obligation is to protect its collection. Anything that threatens the objects must be forbidden.

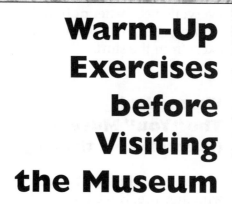

# Warm-Up Exercises before Visiting the Museum

Before going to the museum, prepare young people by limbering them up. Begin by discussing your trip, and talking about what types of things you may be seeing at the museum selected. Then, work through one or more of these warm-up exercises. These exercises establish the tone and type of interaction that will take place at the museum. Consider them to be as important to thinking as stretching is for physical exercise.

Remember to encourage all thoughts and ideas, and to offer some of your own when they are stumped. Continue to wait and ask for more answers after the children feel they have run out. Be patient. Everyone gets better at thinking with practice, but few beginners excel from the start.

## Warm-Up I:
## The "You" Museum
### (fluent/flexible thinking)

Ask your children to think about who they are. Have them consider their individual attributes — what they like, what they dislike, where they live, who they are related to, etc. Have them make a written list of words or phrases they feel could be used to describe who and what they are. Tell them not to stop until they have written down at least 20 descriptive words or phrases. Encourage them to attempt more if they are able. (fluent thinking)

Put the lists aside for a moment, and talk about your museum visit.

Museums are places that collect and display objects relating to themes, such as living creatures, an area's history, the art of Europe and North America, or the lives of people from other cultures. Discuss the type of museum you are going to visit together and the type of things they might be seeing.

Now, tell them that they are going to plan their own museums. This museum's theme is dedicated to them. On the top of another sheet of paper, have them write "The Museum of (their name)." Using the list of words or phrases that are descriptions of themselves, have them think of two objects that would best represent each of their traits or attributes. If they can think of more than two objects, they may list more. (flexible thinking)

Have the children exchange the list of objects, but not the list of traits or attributes, with someone else (or with you if working alone). Have them guess at the meaning of the objects in terms of traits or attributes.

Discuss the variety of ideas that were developed from a single object, and how different some are.

Tell them that objects can be interpreted in more ways than others may have intended.

## Warm-Up 2:
## Time Capsule
### (flexible/original thinking)

Placing objects into a time capsule is a great responsibility. The choices made will reveal to future generations what the world was like during our lifetime.

Have the children determine what objects they might place in a time capsule to tell the future about the present. This can be accomplished as a group or as individuals. Tell them that they are going to be limited by size, and may select no more than 7 objects, none of which can be larger than this book. (flexible thinking)

Now give each child a bonus. Let each one select an 8th object that would be his or her own personal message to future generations. This object may be anything except a written document or letter. (original thinking)

Review the objects that would be in the time capsule. Pretend together that you are people living 200 years from now and you open the capsule. What variety of things could you learn from these objects? Be sure to think of several from each object. (flexible thinking)

## Warm-Up 3:
## Four Questions
### (fluent, flexible, original, and elaborative thinking)

Look at the painting reproduced in this text, or select a painting for a group to view that is easily recognized as having been painted during an earlier time period.

Have everyone use their imaginations to answer the following questions:

1: If this had been painted today, how many things can you think of that would or could be different? (fluent thinking)

2: What other scenes might the artist have painted to give us views of life during his time period? (flexible thinking)

**WOMAN IRONING** - Edgar Degas;
National Gallery of Art,
Washington; Collection of Mr.
and Mrs. Paul Mellon (1882).

3: If you were to paint a scene of
contemporary life, what type of
scene would you paint? (original
thinking)

4: List all the details that might
be in the contemporary painting
you said you would paint in answer
to the previous question. Be sure to
list all the details you can think of.
(elaborative thinking)

# Using the Museum of History or Historic Home

## Introduction

Historic objects are as diverse as history itself, and can be encountered anywhere. An old gramophone could be discovered at a garage sale. A trunk filled with decades-old clothing might be tucked away in the attic. Objects from the past surround us, and need not be found in museums. However, within museums they are displayed in context with other objects of a particular time, giving us a more comprehensive view.

The first museum I ever visited was a museum of local history. I specifically remember an exhibition featuring a family living in my home town during the early 1900's. There was a large photograph of the family having an evening meal together. The table and some of the containers that appeared in the photograph were also exhibited. The son's military uniform was on display, as was the daughter's diary, the father's shaving razor and leather strop, and the mother's hand mirror and brush.

I was most intrigued by the photograph. It seemed as if by looking at their faces I could read their thoughts. The mother looked worried, the father proud. The son, who appeared much too young to wear a uniform, seemed more interested in the food than in having his picture taken. Their daughter looked uncomfortable in her formal clothing.

Not only were these people real, I thought, but had I been living during their time we might have known one another. They could have been my neighbors or even my friends. Seeing their faces and some of their possessions made these people almost familiar.

With great excitement and a sense of discovery, I showed the display to my Mother. She looked amused and began pointing out all that had changed over the years, such as the clothing, the hair styles and the food containers. Though these people had seemed so close to me, they were many years away for her. I had found our similarities, while she had found our differences.

There may be as many ways to appreciate historic objects as there are people to look at them. Just as my Mother and I had approached those objects from our own perspectives, the young people you visit the museum with will bring their own points-of-view to an exploration of objects from other times. That is what creative thinking is all about.

# Activity 1:
# What's the difference?

**Objectives**

This activity challenges young people to think both flexibly and elaboratively as they contemplate the detailed ways our living spaces, and the things contain within them, have changed from an earlier time period to our own.

**Instructions**

This activity works best in a historic home, or a museum that has recreated rooms of a house. Look carefully at the different rooms. Do homes today have these same kinds of rooms? For purposes of this activity, select a room that has a counterpart in our own houses or apartments.

**Activity**

Examine the room together. Make a written inventory of every item it contains.

Now, mentally change that room into a contemporary one. What's the difference? What must change? Next to each item on the inventory, write down those changes that might occur if the room were contemporary. Perhaps the appearance of some objects would change; perhaps

functions would, too. What is the
contemporary room like?
How do these two rooms, the
historic one and the imaginary one,
differ? What might those differences
tell us about each time period?
In what ways has domestic life
changed?

Now try this exercise again.
What changes, other than the ones
listed before, would make the room
or setting contemporary, but in a
different way?

*A creative person will try to
consider things in new and different
ways. Comparing something
unfamiliar with something familiar is
one way to provoke this type of insight.
After considering it as a contemporary
room, do impressions of the historic
room, and the time depicted, change?*

# Activity 2:
# One from all
# and all from one

**Objectives**

This activity calls upon fluent and flexible thinking skills as young people contemplate the range of ideas and products that can evolve from a single starting point.

**Instructions**

An object is considered "antiquated" when it is obsolete, old-fashioned, or out-of-date. As you walk through the history museum, look for those objects surrounding you that are no longer in common use. Then, for purposes of this activity, choose one antiquated item to focus on that is of most interest.

**Activity**

Make a written list of as many functions or purposes served by the antiquated object as can be thought of. Should some assistance in thinking of more than a few functions be required, feel free to read labels, consult text panels in the museum, or ask others for ideas.

Review each of the functions or purposes listed for this antiquated object. Next to each, make a new list of the many other objects used

**Instructions**

This activity is best accomplished with a partner; however, it begins independently. Without partners, stroll through the history museum, noting the location of ten objects that cannot be identified. These objects should be complete mysteries. Participants should be instructed not to read labels, or do anything else to determine what these objects are or what function they may have had. Also, they should not share their selections with anyone else.

**Activity**

Return to those objects selected. Now, think of a "funny or silly" name to give each item. The name might come from its looks, or from an anticipated sound it could make. The name need not be related to the object's true identity or use.

Rewrite each list of objects, scrambling the order. Have partners exchange lists. Go on a hunt, attempting to locate objects you believe match your partner's made-up names. After each of you has selected objects by using the other's list, discuss your selections.

Which names were ascribed to objects other than the ones your partner intended? Which did you identify as your counterpart had? Discuss why choices were made and how connections between names and identities were developed.

This activity can be repeated using attributed "functions" for objects, rather than names.

*Sometimes ideas and possibilities can arise from humor and playfulness. It is important to remember that creative thinking is not necessarily serious business.*

# Activity 4:
# The impact
# of small change

**Objectives**

The purpose of this activity is to provoke fluent, flexible, original and elaborative thinking through response to questions. It is important to develop a quantity of answers, to embellish all answers with detail, and to encourage highly personalized responses.

**Instructions**

As you look at the objects in the historic home or museum of history, try to imagine how different life might have been during the time period the display depicts. Think of

often must make decisions about which items to place on display.

As you look carefully at one gallery within a museum of history, or one room in an historic home, think about why these objects were chosen for display. Consider not only why they might have been chosen, but why they were selected to relate with the other objects in that gallery or room. What might the curator making the selections be trying to tell us?

**Activity**

Together, list all the objects you see in one particular gallery or room. Try not to overlook anything. Next to each item on your list, brainstorm and write down the many ideas or insights the objects provide about events, people, attitudes, values, technologies, etc. of the time period depicted. This will take time and the list will be a long one. Discuss what you learned from the curator's choices.

If you could place one other object in that gallery, what might it be? What would it communicate by itself? What does it communicate in relation to the other things in that space? If you could remove one object from the display, which

would it be? Why did you consider
it expendable or extraneous?
How might the exhibition be
changed by its absence?

As a follow-up activity, have
participants think of one room in
their home as an exhibition of
contemporary history. Have them
list all the objects in that room.
Then, have them write down the
many ideas or insights those objects
reveal about our time period.

If this room in their home were
truly their museum exhibition,
they would probably have more
objects in their collection than
could fit in that room.
What objects might be added to the
room that are not already there, to
better describe our time?
What objects would be removed
from the room, and why?

Now tour the "exhibition" with
its imagined additions and
deletions. What would this
exhibition of contemporary history
tell people living 100 years from
now about our time?

*First and foremost, creativity
happens on a personal level, and
conveys with it individual perspectives*

# Activity 7:
# Coming to your senses

**Objective**

Young people must use both fluent and elaborative thinking as they respond to the challenge of imagining what they can not directly experience in an historic home, or in a museum presenting history exhibitions.

**Instructions**

Toward the conclusion of a visit to an historic home, history museum, or other similar location, gather participants together and have each one select a room or display that was most interesting to them. (Every participant can select a different area or exhibition.) Make certain that each participant names an area out loud.

To make this activity easier, everyone should have paper and pencil.

**Activity**

Have participants close their eyes and picture the room or location they mentioned.
Tell them you want them to make a "visual inventory," picturing everything they saw in that area in their minds. After giving them time to conjure up these images, have them list all these objects on paper.

Next, tell the participants to imagine the *sounds* they might have heard in that same location were they living during the time depicted by the home or display. Make certain that participants do not satisfy this request by merely stating one or two sounds, but that they consider several including those that might be less apparent at first (i.e.- the sounds of a fire in the fireplace or the buzzing of insects in rooms without window screens). Encourage them to refer to their list for ideas.

What *smells* might they notice were they in that location during an earlier time? What would be the sources of those fragrances and aromas? Again, don't allow participants to be satisfied with the first answer that comes to mind. Have them strive to think of others by referring to their lists.

Next, explore the *feel* of the objects in the room. Would chairs, beds, or other pieces of furniture be hard or soft, comfortable or uncomfortable? What about utensils, fabrics, and fixtures? Have participants use their inventory lists to describe the many textures they might touch (such as

more than just a physical description of their activities. Ask them to embellish their descriptions with personal impressions or emotional responses to each situation.

Remember, you want participants to use their elaborative thinking, so get them to incorporate and account for as many details in their descriptions as possible. A good way to encourage this is by asking lots of follow-up questions.

*Creative people do more than just imagine things. They bring ideas to life by considering their many details and aspects. How different do you think your life would be if you had to remain in the time period you just investigated?*

# Using the Science Museum

## Introduction

For many of us, science is an exclusive domain of facts and figures that we do not know. It is a convergent discipline that seeks correct answers and exact measurements. Science, after all, explains things.

While convergence is a necessary and important aim of science, scientific investigations are particularly reliant upon divergent thinking. Scientists consistently

**Activity**

This activity begins with a hunt to locate an object that measures something. What is the function of the measurement device selected? Read labels or ask museum personnel if there are questions about the device, how it is used, or what it measures.

If you were allowed to use this device for a day, how many things could you measure with it? Make as complete a list as possible.

Now, think of some other method to measure the items on your list, if the device selected were not available. Include as many other ways as you can possibly think of.

*Creativity often involves the ability to devise a variety of ways to accomplish something. From what you discovered in this activity, how could you develop your own tool for making measurements?*

## Activity 2:
## Striking a match

**Objectives**

As they develop and use categories of their own for grouping facts and information, participants will stimulate their flexible and elaborative thinking abilities.

**Instructions**

In order to make sense out of many objects or facts, we group like things together. This is called classifying. If you collect stamps, or coins, or almost anything else, you probably classify your collection, putting like items together.

Some stores classify what they sell into departments, grouping men's clothes together, cosmetics together, household items together, and so forth.

Newspapers classify personal advertisements together to make shopping for a new car, job or pet easier.

Scientists attempt to group like things or facts together, too, in order to make information more meaningful. In this activity you will develop your own system of classification.

in most museums that are not exclusively life sciences.

An invention is often the clever combination of two seemingly disparate existing things. An alarm clock combined with a radio gave us the radio alarm clock and a musical way to awaken in the morning. Wheels were put together with a chair to create the wheelchair, assisting people who are mobility-impaired. And when a tabletop was used as the court on which to play an indoor game of tennis, "Ping Pong," or table tennis was invented.

**Activity**

Select 20 objects in the museum at random. Make two lists of 10 objects each on the left and right sides of your paper. Draw a line from an object on one list to an object on the other list.

The two objects connected by your lines are the objects participants must combine to make an invention. Have everyone try making various fanciful combinations of each set of two objects. Ask participants to write down what their most promising inventions are, and how they are used. Each person should have developed at least 10 inventions by the end of this activity.

*Though this activity was fanciful, many inventions were once the product of fantasies. Consider Leonardo da Vinci's helicopter or Jules Verne's submarine. Just because the technology to develop an idea is not available at the time does not mean that the idea is without merit.*

# Activity 4:
# Wearing different hats

This activity serves to provoke fluent, flexible and elaborative thinking by requiring an examination of a single object from the concerns and vantage points of various disciplines.

**Objectives**

"Science" is a large and encompassing term that refers to many areas or disciplines. For purposes of this exercise, it is useful to think of science as composed of three main branches.They are: (1) the life sciences, (2) the physical sciences, and (3) the social sciences.

**Instructions**

The life sciences involve the study of living organisms.

Notice the differences and overlap between your three lists, detailing various approaches to the same object. Now, to challenge you from a very different direction, make a final list of how you might investigate this object wearing the hat of an artist.

*Look again at the original list of reasons you were interested in the object selected. How many of your reasons reflected the concerns of life, physical or social science perspectives? How many reflected the concerns of an artist? Creative thinkers take advantage of diverse perspectives when attempting to gain new or alternative approaches and insights.*

## Activity 5: Possible and improbable answers

**Objectives**

Fluent and flexible thinking are required to develop a list of possible and improbable answers to questions about a scientific object or specimen.

**Instructions**

If a cup were to suddenly fly across the room, you would want to know how it happened. You would immediately begin trying to think of as many answers to the riddle of "the flying cup" as you could. Your answers might range from those that seem possible and sensible, to those too improbable to readily accept.

Creating a list of possible and improbable answers to a puzzling question is similar to constructing a scientific hypothesis, or educated guess. You consider many possibilities, even ones that might be popularly rejected, before establishing your best guess as to the real answer.

In similar fashion this activity challenges you to develop answers, ranging from possible to improbable, to questions posed about an object in the science museum.

This activity may be accomplished alone or with others.

**Activity**

Locate an object that you, and any partners working with you, are not familiar with. Using your powers of observation and imagination, think of as many possible, improbable, and even foolish answers to each

where it is located. Read the list of descriptions you have been given. Develop a mental picture of what the object or specimen described looks like.

Now, draw a picture of the object or specimen as described by your partner. Draw it as described, even if you feel that the description may not fit with what you believe the object to be.

Before exchanging drawings, have your partner take you to the object he or she described. After seeing what the object or specimen actually is, reveal your drawing.

How closely matched are the drawing and the objects? Explain the interpretations that may have lead to any differences.

*Each of us perceives things differently, through our own perspectives, priorities and interests. The creative thinker is aware of this, and consciously uses these differences to his or her advantage.*

# Activity 7:
# What a pair might share

Using fluent, flexible, and elaborative thinking, participants must consider the numerous similarities and differences in two different life forms.

**Objectives**

This activity works best in a zoo where living creatures can be seen and their behaviors observed, or in a museum of natural history, where mounted specimens are available for inspection.

**Instructions**

The goal of this exercise is to compare and contrast two life forms. Should only one life form be available, or should participants prefer, comparisons can be made to human beings.

Participants should be assigned a life form to observe and describe. Paper and pencil are needed. If only one young person is participating, you should serve as his or her partner.

The piece of paper supplied to participants should be divided into two columns. The columns should be headed with the words,

**Activity**

common?  How many differences can they discover?

With older participants, this activity might continue with discussions about some other relationships these two life forms share.  For instance, are they both mammals, reptiles, amphibians, or insects?  Are they both nocturnal or diurnal?  Are they both herbivores, carnivores, or omnivores?

*Creative people learn by making comparisons.  Their highly developed observation skills permit them to make discoveries by contrasting one thing or behavior to another. Could you think of as many similiarities as dissimiliarities?*

# Activity 8:
# Breaking it down

**Objective**

The purpose of this activity is to exercise elaborative thinking, while sharpening participants' observations skills.

**Instructions**

This exercise is appropriate for use with any animal or plant, regardless of the setting or institution in which it appears. It works best, however, if accomplished in a museum's, zoo's, or garden's "discovery area," where young people are permitted to touch, inspect, and even dismantle a specimen.

Provide participants with paper and crayons or colored pencils. Allowing participants to use a magnifying glass gives them another way to inspect their specimens and gather visual information.

**Activity**

Scientists must be aware of every part of an animal or plant. Each part they can identify has importance, and each could serve a purpose that helps scientists understand it, and our world, better. But, before each part can be investigated, each must be isolated and noted.

Participants should be provided with an individual specimen, such as a flower, fruit, or skeletal remains to inspect. (Before they begin to investigate their specimen, this activity might be modeled by you or a member of the institution visited.)

Each young person should be asked to note all of the parts of the specimen they received. Since most of the names of these parts will be unknown to the participants, have them make drawings and/or write out elaborate descriptions of each part they isolate. If using magnifying glasses, prompt the participants to use the magnifying glasses, afterward, to break down all the components into even smaller components.

At the conclusion of this exercise, have the participants share all that they discovered with the rest of the group. An appropriate follow-up would be asking the participants to look up the specimen they investigated in reference texts. Have them find the names of each part they identified.

*Elaborative thinkers notice details. Did you begin to see more as you began investigating? Did using a magnifying glass lead you to find more components? What do you think you might have found if you could have also used a microscope?*

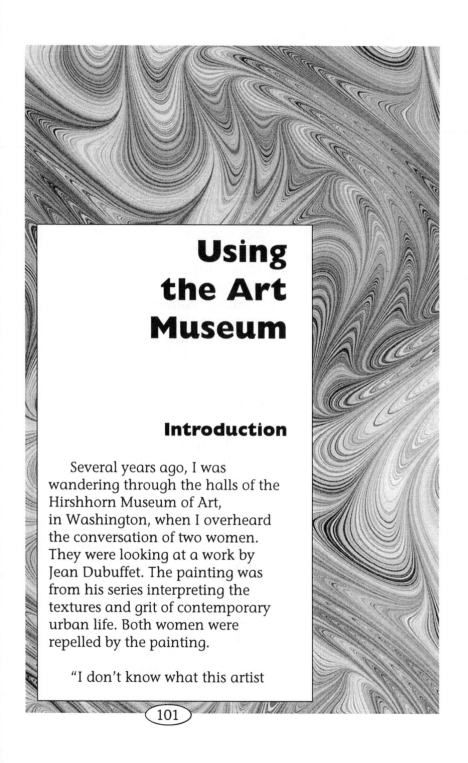

# Using the Art Museum

## Introduction

Several years ago, I was wandering through the halls of the Hirshhorn Museum of Art, in Washington, when I overheard the conversation of two women. They were looking at a work by Jean Dubuffet. The painting was from his series interpreting the textures and grit of contemporary urban life. Both women were repelled by the painting.

"I don't know what this artist

was trying to do," said one of the women, "but the painting looks filthy to me."

"It's as though he painted a picture of grime," the other responded in disgust and they both immediately moved on.

Each came away from that experience feeling as though she had missed the meaning of that painting, yet each had understood it. Dubuffet's painting had communicated beautifully, not in the only way it might, but in an intended way. Yet they lacked the self-confidence to trust in their own response mechanisms and perceptions. Their self-concept made them incapable of trusting what they had come to understand almost instantaneously. I am certain that had an "expert" told them those same things they would have found the painting more interesting, and would have more fully trusted the interpretation.

One does not need "expert" assistance to use the art museum to enhance creativity. Works of art provide us with points-of-departure for our insights and imaginings.

As perfume reacts differently to each individual's personal chemistry, thus having a slightly different fragrance on each person wearing it, art provokes different responses in each individual viewing it. We react **with** art, not simply to it. Therefore, one person's view of art, for purposes of stimulating creativity, is as valid as anyone else's.

# Activity 1:
# Metaphorically speaking

**Objectives**

The purpose of this activity is to challenge fluent thinking skills. Similes and metaphors are used because they help make comparisons between something we understand and something we are trying to understand. By the end of this activity, participants will have thought of as many comparisons as possible, and have found numerous ways to consider, a non-representational work of art.

**Instructions**

Metaphors and similes are used frequently in everyday conversations. They provide us with ways of drawing comparisons between two things that are not alike. Metaphors draw the

comparison in very closely.
They do not even tell you that they
are making a comparison.
"He's a bad apple," is a metaphor.
Similes do the same thing,
only they tell you that a
comparison is being made.
"He is like a bad apple because once
he starts being bad he just gets
worse." Similes use the words "like"
or "as" in their comparisons;
metaphors do not.

**Activity**

Select a work of art that is non-
representational (that does not look
like something recognizable).
Spend several minutes just looking
at it. Ask everyone to "see" as many
of its qualities and features as
possible.

After you feel that they have
had time to familiarize themselves
with the work, ask for metaphors or
similes that are parallel to it.
For example, "This sculpture is a
fortress," or "This sculpture is like
crumpled paper, full of folds and
edges."

Have the participants make as
many metaphors and similes as
they can. These comparisons can
refer to the entire piece or just to
one detail. The point is to think of

as many as possible. Do not stop
until they have run out of ideas for
at least a few minutes. Remember
to keep asking for more.

When they haven't been able to
think of any other metaphors or
similes for some time, change
position in relationship to that
work. Perhaps they might step very
close to it, or very far from it.
If it is sculpture, walk to the other
side of it, or view it from the top,
down, or bottom, up. See if they
can't continue to find metaphors or
similes when viewing the work from
this new vantage point.

*Think about how many ways they
developed to approach this art work;
how they described it and related it to
other ideas and things. Creative
thinking techniques can help you
approach and relate to objects, ideas
and problems that may, at first, seem
unapproachable.*

# Activity 2:
# Token response

[This activity was originally developed by Eldon Katter and Terri Kriebel of Kutztown College and has been adapted for this text.]

**Objectives**

This activity stimulates flexible, original and elaborative thinking by encouraging young people to look at things using a variety of criteria. It will also acquaint them with some of the differences between "preferences" (I like it) and "judgments" (it is good). By the end of this activity, participants will have considered works of art from many perspectives, and have learned a few of the many criteria that can be used to evaluate a work of art.

**Instructions**

With a writing tablet in hand, walk through the art museum until you come to a gallery that has diverse types or styles of art. It is best to use a gallery containing works by more than one or two artists. If not available, choose a gallery containing more than 10 pieces. After locating this type of gallery, spend time looking carefully at all the works in the room. Get to know each one.

## Activity

For purposes of this exercise, works of art may be used or selected as many times as you wish. Though this activity can be accomplished alone, it works very well with groups. When working in groups do not let participants share their selections with others until instructed to do so. Remember, there are no right or wrong answers to these questions or considerations.

1: In their notebooks or writing tablets, have each participant write down the name of the art work in this gallery that they like the best. Beside its title, draw a heart. Have them list the reasons they like it best.

2: Sometimes we are interested in how much money works of art cost. Have them choose, individually, the piece that they feel costs the most money. Beside its title, draw a dollar sign ($). Have them jot notes down telling why they feel that this work costs the most.

3: How much time does it take to make a work of art? There needs to be time to develop the idea, time to execute the idea, time devoted to craftsmanship, etc. Which piece in this gallery do you think took the most time to produce?

Have participants draw a clock by the title of this work and make notes to tell why they feel it took so much more time than the others.

4: Not everyone likes the same things. For adults, which piece of art do you think a child would prefer? For children, which piece do you think an adult or parent would like best? Write down the name of the person you are thinking of next to the title of the work. List the reasons why you think that person would choose that particular piece.

5: If a group of famous art critics, who know lots about art, were going to choose the best piece and award it a prize, which would it be? Draw a blue ribbon next to this work's title. Remember to write down all the reasons why art critics would select that work.

6: We can prefer some pieces. We can judge certain works to be good, but we don't have to value everything. Which piece do you like least? Write down the title and next to it write the word "YUK!" Remember to list the reasons why you do not care for this work.

If you are working with a group, go back over each selection. Discuss why each of you selected the pieces you did for each criteria. Feel free to talk about the differences and similarities of reasons and choices.

If working with one participant, consider how many criteria he or she used to make decisions about the works.

Whether with one participant or a group, possible discussion topics include:

> Pieces attracting a wide variety of criteria;
> Pieces attracting little or no attention;
> Reasons for choosing certain pieces;
> How reasons differ using different criteria;
> What other criteria could have been used.

*Think about how many ways there are to appreciate, value or just consider something. Why is it better to postpone deciding how you feel about things until after you consider them from a variety of vantage points? What did this exercise tell you about approaching other problems or situations?*

# Activity 3:
# Forced fit

**Objectives**

The purpose of "Forced Fit" is to stimulate flexible and original thinking. By the end of this activity participants will have had to view an art work for an extended period of time, think of its attributes, and consider it from an "unnatural" point of view in order to understand it in different ways.

**Instructions**

Before selecting an object to focus upon, spend time thinking of all the attributes and qualities of a "cat." Consider a cat in as many ways as possible. On a tablet, write down a list of everything you can think of. Remember to ask everyone to use all their senses. Here are a few to get you started: agile, curved, soft, lazy, mysterious...

**Activity**

Locate an art work (painting, photograph, sculpture, etc.) that interests everyone. Think about what drew them to it. Have participants make a few notes to themselves on what drew them to this particular art work.

Now, consider that work of art using your list of the attributes and qualities of a cat. For example: This painting is "soft like a cat" where the artist made the sky and water meet; or: This painting is "curved like a cat" when your eye follows these lines and those shapes.

See how many ways they can tie in the attributes of a cat to the art work. If you are working in a group, allow everyone to say their ideas without judgment. It is fine to build upon an idea presented by someone else.

After they can find no more ways to connect the two unconnected things, have everyone look back at the notes made about being drawn to this piece. What draws their attention now? Do they think of the work differently? How?

*Ideas can come from the strangest places. A seemingly disconnected thought or activity can sometimes lead to very useful insights. How can you apply this principle to "real life" problems?*

## Activity 4: Reversal

**Objectives**

This activity is designed to provoke flexible and elaborative thinking. By the end of this activity, young people will have had to consider a work of art that does not appeal to their aesthetic tastes and develop a different value system by which to judge it. In addition, they will have become more observant of detail.

**Instructions**

As you roam through the galleries of the museum, pay special attention to those works of art that you feel are most inaccessible to (least understandable) or are most uncomfortable (least pleasing to aesthetic tastes). After you have noted several, return to the one that evoked the strongest negative response.

**Activity**

Spend a few moments examining the work of art selected. Without regard to what they like or dislike, attempt to survey all its component details, such as: use of color, textures, shapes, rhythm, subject matter, etc.

With the presumption in mind that they have selected this work because they do not like it, ask them to try and find one redeeming feature. This is not unlike trying to find a redeeming feature in someone whose company you feel less than comfortable with. Perhaps it is the way brushstrokes convey emotion; or perhaps the way in which colors seem to work against one another.

Now find as many more redeeming features as you can. After you have "pushed" to develop a list of as many redeeming features as possible, take another look at this work by considering these questions:

1: Was the artist able to communicate with viewers?

2: Since we presume that the communication and the message were intentional, were they successful? If yes, why; if not, why not?

3: Why do you believe the artist chose to communicate using the images he/she used? What images might have been more successful; what images might have been less successful?

4: If you were giving a tour of the museum and brought visitors to this art work, what would you say about it to give the visitors a balanced (fair and objective) view of the piece?

*Sometimes we are far too ready to reject thoughts or ideas or activities because we disagree with them, or feel that they are bad. Though we are entitled to our point of view, what can be learned by spending time considering something that we might ordinarily dismiss?*

# Activity 5:
# Art critic

**Objectives**

This activity will call upon an ability to think fluently, flexibly, and elaboratively. By the end of this activity, participants will have used standards set by the execution of one art work to consider another. They will determine, in detail, all that would have to change if one art work were to conform to the style and execution of another.

**Instructions**

Examine carefully a work of art that has a realistic appearance. Note as many things about it as you can, from what is depicted, to colors, style, and placement of things within the composition.

Jot down everything you can classify or categorize about this piece. This work, and everything it does, will serve as your standard of excellence for works of art.
Whether you personally like this work or not, for purposes of this exercise, this work will be considered perfect.

Now select a work by a different artist. Go through your list from the previous art work examined, and compare the characteristics of the first piece to that of the second. If the first piece is the standard of excellence by which the second is to be judged, what has the artist of the second work done correctly, and what has he/she executed incorrectly? Develop as long a list as possible for both. Now go back over what the artist of the second work did incorrectly. What would he/she have to change about the art work to make it as "excellent" as the first is?

*What effects do preconceived ideas have upon our problem-solving abilities? What new insights are possible when we decide to re-evaluate something, or challenge a way of thinking, using different standards?*

**Activity**

# Activity 6:
# It's written
# all over their faces

**Objectives**

Looking at portraiture can be monotonous. After viewing a gallery of portraits, they often seem repetitive, or simply uninteresting because we know nothing about the people we are looking at.
By the end of this exercise, participants will have used original and elaborative thinking to make some determinations about the people depicted in portraits, and will have developed their own ideas/stories about who these people were and what they were like.

**Instructions**

Locate a gallery filled with portraiture, if one is available to you. If not, note the location of four or more portraits that you can use for this activity. Spend time getting "acquainted" with each of the portraits you choose. Be very observant. Strive to notice everything you can about the subject of the portrait.
Be certain to pay attention to "clues" provided about the person portrayed (objects in background, the clothing, facial expressions,

and so forth). Do not read labels or titles.

    Before you spend time trying to know who these people actually were, why not make up lives and reputations for them based on what they look like, what they are pictured with, and how the artist portrays them? In almost every portrait are clues as to the artist's feelings about his or her subject. It may be the turn of the mouth or the bend of a sleeve. Make up stories about these people. Try to determine as much about them as imaginations permit. Think of it as though describing the characters in your own "soap opera." Remember, the point is not to guess correctly, but to use the portrait as a point of departure to develop an elaborate story of your own making.

*Creative thinkers explore ideas and objects in depth. Examining details to gain new insights and imaginings is one way to "see" more. How did your thoughts change as you moved from looking at the overview to examining the details?*

**Activity**

# Activity 7: Lots o' lines

**Objectives**

The goal of of this activity is to prompt young people to use their fluent, flexible and elaborative thinking using an exercise that easily adapts in its level of sophistication to most age groups.

**Instructions**

Lines are one of the most basic design elements artists use to translate their ideas into images. This activity requires the participants to identify as many lines as possible within each work of art they inspect. The activity works best if many works of art are used for this purpose.

Before beginning, introduce this activity by having participants recall the "lines" they saw on the way to art museum. Most probably they saw lines on the street; lines made by bricks and wood on buildings; the lines created by tree limbs; the lines made by fences; lines of cars in traffic; and so forth.

Next, have participants brainstorm the many ways lines are made. These ways include: by a pencil, with a paintbrush, by carving or cutting, by the edges of things, where shadows and light meet, at the horizon, by ripples in water, at the corners of rooms where walls meet, etc.

**Activity**

After conducting the introduction to this activity as mentioned above, tell participants that their challenge is to see as many lines as possible in each art work that you view together. As you arrive at a painting, sculpture, photograph, or other work of art, ask the youngsters to look for a moment without saying anything. Tell them to use this quiet time to find as *many* lines as possible.

Prior to asking for their responses, remind participants that, when attempting to point out the lines they see, they should not get close enough to the art to alert the guards or endanger the work. Then, have participants point out every type of line they can see in the art. Older children might be challenged to tell the others how the lines they identify were made.

*Did you discover more and more lines as you continued to look at an art work? Sometimes, solving problems or seeing new things requires spending more time and working harder. Creative people are willing to continue trying long after others have given up.*

# Activity 8: Decorated people

**Objectives**

This activity is designed to prompt young people to think flexibly and elaboratively as they make connections between practices that are familar and those that are not.

**Instructions**

Use this activity in museums presenting the art of other cultures, such as Pre-Columbian, African, Oceanic, Native American, Eskimo, or Asian. This activity serves to make unfamiliar customs seem less strange by connecting them to behaviors and practices that are more familiar. Due to the complex connections that must be made, this activity is most suitable for participants of 12 years or older.

**Activity**

Begin by asking participants to name some of the many things people in our culture do to enhance their appearance. Answers will range from make-up to hair removal, contact lenses to tattoos, and from nail polish to cosmetic surgery. After each answer is offered, attempt to restate it in a manner that makes it sound less familiar or "acceptable."

For example, if a young person offers the answer "ear piercing," respond by agreeing that we do poke holes in our ears so that decorative objects can be hung near our faces. Or, if someone says "braces on teeth," say "yes, we do use metal clamps that are slowly tightened to move teeth into a more pleasing arrangement."

Next, look at the objects in the museum. At each representation of a human figure, face mask, or each piece of adornment worn by humans, ask participants to draw parallels to some of those things we do to ourselves. For instance, scarification might be equated with tattooing or make-up, or blackened teeth could be seen as similar to having teeth capped or painting one's finger and toe nails.

*Creative people realize that there will be differences among people and the ways they express themselves. Most do not think of this as threatening or wrong. Rather, they appreciate those differences as interesting, and try to understand them better. Did you gain an appreciation for the culture whose objects you looked at by doing this activity?*

# Conclusion

## What happens next?

We exercise our divergent thinking to strengthen the "tool" used when confronting problems, questions or things. This tool serves as a pry, opening our creativity and giving us access to a fuller range of possibilities, alternatives, options, or consequences before establishing limits or making choices.

This text challenged participants to practice divergent thinking within museum settings. Museums are ideally suited for this because they present high-caliber stimuli, in great numbers and proximity to one another, far from a context where risk-taking involves "real"

consequences from peers,
co-workers, teachers, or family.

Divergent thinking can and
should be part of an approach to
problem-solving wherever it occurs.
The activities in this book,
for example, need not be restricted
to objects found in museums.
They can be used almost anywhere
with nearly anything. They do not
even have to be divided by subject
matter. The activities under history,
for example, could be adapted for
art or science.

We apply divergent thinking for
the purpose of *generating ideas and
possibilities, beyond the function of
habit and opinion, in order to achieve
personal discovery, change and a
higher level of understanding.*
In other words, to be more creative.

# Won't lots of ideas just confuse the issue?

Several things happen when we seek alternatives and possibilities.
We identify new ways of approaching a problem.
We gain new perspectives.
We may actually solve the problem using a new idea generated.
And, even if our search proves less than productive, we develop the discipline of seeking options rather than routinely following the dictates of habit or opinion.

Divergent thinking gives us the freedom to choose among options.
Remember, our search for alternatives does not in any way prevent us from returning to our first idea or usual response.
It simply gives us the opportunity to do otherwise should it prove productive or useful.

## How do we tackle problems divergently when they are not accompanied by games or exercises?

When encountering a problem or challenge, we have learned that new ideas, insights and imaginings can be brought forth by asking ourselves questions before satisfying ourselves with answers.
The questions we ask can be designed to provoke four types of thinking associated with creativity. They are: fluency, flexibility, originality and elaboration.

If a quantity of ideas or possibilities are important, fluent thinking is required.
Questions that begin with "how many different . . ." will stimulate this mode of thought.

When it is useful to consider a wide range of alternatives to one single approach or outcome, flexible thinking can help.
To provoke this type of thinking, ask questions that begin,
"in what other ways..."
or "how else might..."

Should a highly personalized response or solution be called for, original thinking is needed.
Try asking "what might I/you..." or "how would I/you..."
Allow ideas to reflect differences in personalities, interests, and perspectives.

When more information is needed, or more detailed thought is essential, focus on elaborative thinking. "Identify all the aspects of..." or "tell more about..." are the types of questions that can stimulate this mode of thinking.

## As creative abilities are applied to problems that are not games or exercises, what should be kept in mind?

In his book *A Whack on the Side of the Head*, Roger von Oech says, "We learn by trial and error, not by trial and rightness."
This is not only clever, it is important. Creative thinkers allow themselves to try, without expecting

that each attempt will result in success.

Whether working to develop an idea or attempting to solve a personal problem, the search for possibilities will, by necessity, generate vast numbers of inappropriate alternatives. However, by generating and sorting through alternatives, we gain a broader perspective, teach ourselves resourcefulness, and discover routes for expressing our own individuality.

With practice and patience we can begin to derive as much pleasure and satisfaction from the process of thinking creatively, as from reaping its rewards.

# Bibliography

Adams, James L. *The Care and Feeding of Ideas: A Guide to Encouraging Creativity*. Reading, MA: Addison-Wesley, 1986.

Albrecht, Karl. *Brain Building: Easy Games to Develop Your Problem-Solving Skills*. New York: Prentice-Hall, 1984.

Albrecht, Karl. *Brain Power: Learn to Improve Your Thinking Skills*. Englewood Cliffs, NJ: Prentice-Hall, 1980.

Allen, Henry. "Announcing (Are You Ready?) the Latest Trend: Thinking." *Seattle Times*, Seattle, WA, May 15, 1988, pp. A16-17.

Baron, Joan Boykoff, and Robert J. Sternberg, eds. *Teaching Thinking Skills: Theory and Practice*. New York: W.H. Freeman and Company, 1987.

Berger, Joseph. "Classroom Focus Shifting to the Art of Thinking." *The New York Times*, New York, NY, April 13, 1988, p. Y23.

Bingham, Alma. *Improving Children's Facility in Problem Solving*. New York: Teachers College, Columbia University, 1963.

Biondi, Angelo, ed. *The Creative Process*. Buffalo, NY: D.O.K. Publishers, 1972.

de Bono, Edward. *Lateral Thinking: Creativity Step by Step*. New York: Harper and Row, 1970.

Boorstin, Daniel. "History Teaches 'We Don't Know What We Think We Know.'" *U.S. News & World Report*, March 5, 1984, p. 73.

Bronowski, Jacob. *The Origins of Knowledge and Imagination*. New Haven, CT: Yale University Press, 1978.

Buyer, Linda S. "Creative Problem Solving: A Comparison of Performance Under Different Instructions." *The Joural of Creative Bahavior*, Vol. 22, No. 1 (First Quarter, 1988), pp. 55-61.

Carnegie Symposium on Creativity. *Creativity: A Continuing Inventory of Knowledge by The Council of Scholars of The Library of Congress*, November 19-20, 1981, James H. Hutson, ed. Washington, DC: Library of Congress, 1981.

Davis, Gary A., and Joseph A. Scott, eds. *Training Creative Thinking*. Huntington, NY: Robert E. Krieger Publishing Company, 1978.

Fabun, Don. *Communications: The Transfer of Meaning.* Beverly Hills, CA: Glencoe Press, 1968.

Feldhusen, John, ed. *Toward Excellence in Gifted Education.* Denver, CO: Love Publishing, 1985.

Fernald, Lloyd W., Jr. "Values and Creativity." *The Journal of Creative Behavior,* Vol. 21, No. 4 (Fourth Quarter, 1987), pp. 312-324.

Gartenhaus, Alan Reid. *In Pursuit of Wild Geese, Teaching Creative Thinking: A Smithsonian Approach.* Washington, DC: Smithsonian Institution, 1984.

Gartenhaus, Alan Reid. "Museums and Critical Thinking Skills for Students." Washington, DC: Smithsonian Institution, 1983, (mimeographed).

Getty Center for Education in the Arts. *Discipline-Based Art Education: What Forms Will It Take?* Proceedings of a National Invitational Conference. January 15-17, 1987, pp. 80-95.

Gingerich, Owen, ed. *Scientific Genuis and Creativity: Readings from Scientific American.* New York: W.H. Freeman and Company, 1982.

Grinder, Allison L., and E. Sue McCoy. *The Good Guide: A Sourcebook for Interpreters, Docents, and Tour Guides.* Scottsdale, AZ: Ironwood Press, 1985.

Guilford, J.P. *The Nature of Human Intelligence.* New York: McGraw-Hill, 1967.

Hahn, Jon. "Closing Off Creativity." *Seattle Post-Intelligencer,* February 12, 1989, p. F1.

Isakson, Scott G., and Donald J. Treffinger. *Creative Problem Solving: The Basic Course.* Buffalo, NY: Bearly Limited, 1985.

Kantrowitz, Barbara, and Pat Wingert. "How Kids Learn." *Newsweek,* April 17, 1989, pp. 50-57.

Katter, Eldon, and Terri Kriebel. "Token Response: A Lesson in Response to the Arts." Kutztown, PA: 1982, (mimeographed).

Lubeck, Sally, and Thomas Bidell. "Creativity and Cognition: A Piagetian Framework." *The Journal of Creative Behavior,* Vol. 22, No. 1 (First Quarter, 1988), pp. 31-41.

MacKinnon, D.W. *In Search of Human Effectiveness.* Buffalo, NY: Creative Education Foundation, 1978.

Morgan, Bruce. "In Massachusetts: Boffo Science." *Time Magazine,* April 4, 1988, pp. 10, H1, 11.

Nierenberg, Gerald I. *The Art of Creative Thinking.* New York: Simon and Schuster, 1982.

Olson, Robert W. *The Art of Creative Thinking: A Practical Guide.* New York: Barnes and Noble, 1980.

Parnes, Sidney J. "Visioneering — State of the Art." *The Journal of Creative Behavior,* Vol. 21, No. 4 (Fourth Quarter, 1987), pp. 283-299.

Perkins, D.N. *The Mind's Best Work.* Cambridge, MA: Harvard University Press, 1981.

Popham, W. James, and Eva L. Baker. *Establishing Instructional Goals.* Englewood Cliffs, NJ: Prentice-Hall, 1970.

Prince, George M. *The Practice of Creativity: A Manual for Dynamic Group Problem Solving.* New York: Harper and Row, 1970, p. 188.

Shavelson, R.J., J.J. Hubner, and J.C. Stanton. "Self-Concept: Validation of Construct Interpretations." *Review of Educational Research*, Vol. 46, 1976, pp. 407-441.

Torrance, E. Paul. *Education and the Creative Potential.* Minnespolis, MN: University of Minnesota Press, 1963.

Tyler, L.E. *Individual Differences: Abilities and Motivational Directions.* New York: Prentice-Hall, 1982.

Van Gundy, Arthur B. *Training Your Creative Mind.* Englewood Cliffs, NJ: Prentice-Hall, 1982.

Vaughan, Trefor. "On Not Predicting the Outcome: Creativity as Adventure." *The Journal of Creative Behavior*, Vol. 21, No. 4 (Fourth Quarter, 1987), pp. 300-311.

von Oech, Roger. *A Whack on the Side of the Head: How to Unlock Your Mind for Innovation.* New York: Warner Books, 1983.

Williams, Robert H., and John Stockmyer. *Unleashing the Right Side of the Brain: The LARC Creativity Program.* Lexington, MA: The Stephen Greene Press, 1987.

Young, Robert E., ed. *Fostering Critical Thinking*. San Francisco, CA: Jossey-Bass, 1980.

# List of Museums

The list of museums which follows is offered as a convenience, and as an initial starting point for locating museums in your area, or in travel destinations.
Inclusion in this list is not meant as a recommendation for use; likewise omission from this list should not be considered a lack of endorsement.

Many local colleges and universities will have art, history and science museums or galleries open to the general public.
In addition, most museum personnel will be pleased to direct you to other facilities in their vicinity if you inquire.

This list was derived from *The Official Museum Directory* (National Register Publishing Co., Wilmette, IL, 1989), a valuable reference listing over 6,600 museums, and suppliers of more than 50 types of museum products and services. For more information call 1-800-323-6772.

# History Museums and Historic Homes

## Alabama

Alabama Department of Archives & History
624 Washington Ave.
Montgomery, AL 36130
(205) 261-4361

Historic Mobile Preservation Society
300 Oakleigh Pl.
Mobile, AL 36604
(205) 432-6161

## Alaska

Alaska State Museum
395 Whittier
Juneau, AK 99801
(907) 465-2901

Anchorage Museum of History and Art
121 W. 7th Ave.
Anchorage, AK 99501
(907) 343-4326

Klondike Gold Rush National Historical Park
2nd & Broadway
Skagway, AK 99840
(907) 983-2921

## Arizona

Arizona Historical Society
949 E. 2nd St.
Tucson, AZ 85719
(602) 628-5774

Museum of Northern Arizona
Fort Valley Rd.
Flagstaff, AZ 86001
(602) 774-5211

Pioneer Arizona Living History Museum
Pioneer Rd.
Phoenix, AZ 85027
(602) 993-0212

Tempe Historical Museum
3500 S. Rural Rd.
Tempe, AZ 85282
(602) 350-5100

## Arkansas

Arkansas Museum of Science and History
MacArthur Park
Little Rock, AR 72202
(501) 371-3521

Miles Musical
Museum
Highway 62 W.
Eureka Springs, AR
72632
(501) 253-8961

The Old
State House
300 W. Markham
St.
Little Rock, AR
72201
(501) 371-1749

Rosalie House
282 Spring St.
Eureka Springs, AR
72632
(501) 253-7377

## California

Clarke Memorial
Museum
240 E St.
Eureka, CA 95501
(707) 443-1947

Fowler Museum
of Cultural History
University
of California
Los Angeles, CA
90024
(213) 825-4361

National Maritime
Museum
Hyde Street Pier
San Francisco, CA
94109
(415) 556-3002

Nevada County
Historical Society,
Inc.
Nevada City, CA
(916) 265-5468

The Oakland
Museum
1000 Oak St.
Oakland, CA 94607
(415) 273-3401

## Colorado

Aspen Historical
Society Museum
620 Bleeker
Aspen, CO 81611
(303) 925-3721

Colorado Springs
Pioneers Museum
215 S. Tejon
Colorado Springs,
CO 80903
(719) 578-6650

El Pueblo Museum
905 S. Prarie Ave.
Pueblo, CO 81005
(719) 564-5274

Greeley Municipal
Museum
919 7th St.
Greeley, CO 80631
(303) 350-9220

The Molly Brown
House & Museum
1340 Pennsylvania
St.
Denver, CO 80203
(303) 832-4092

Museum
of Western
Colorado
248 S. 4th St.
Grand Junction, CO
81501
(303) 242-0971

State Historical
Society
of Colorado
1300 Broadway
Denver, CO 80203
(303) 866-5739

## Connecticut

Connecticut
Historical Society
1 Elizabeth St.
Hartford, CT 06106
(203) 236-5621

Fairfield Historical
Society
636 Old Post Rd.
Fairfield, CT 06430
(203) 259-1598

Mark Twain
Memorial
351 Framington
Ave.
Hartford, CT 06105
(203) 247-0998

Museum of Art,
Science
and Industry
4450 Park Ave.
Bridgeport, CT
06604
(203) 372-3521

Mystic Seaport
50 Greenmanville
Ave.
Mystic, CT 06355
(203) 572-0711

## Delaware

Bureau
of Museums
and Historic Sites
102 S. State St.
Dover, DE 19903
(302) 736-5316

Delaware
Agricultural
Museum
866 N. Dupont
Hwy.
Dover, DE 19901
(302) 734-1618

Winterthur
Museum
Rt. 52
Winterthur, DE
19735
(302) 888-4600

# District
# of Columbia

Dumbarton Oaks
House, Library,
& Collection
2715 Q St., NW
Washington, DC
20007
(202) 342-3200

Meridian House
International
1630 Crescent Pl.,
NW
Washington, DC
20009
(202) 667-6800

The Octagon
1799 New York
Ave., NW
Washington, DC
20006
(202) 638-3105

Smithsonian
Institution
(collection
of history, science,
art, and air/space
museums)
1000 Jefferson Dr.
Washington, DC
20560
(202) 357-1300

The White House
1600 Pennsylvania
Ave., NW
Washington, DC
20500
(202) 456-1414

# Florida

Edison Winter
Home
and Museum
2350 McGregor
Blvd.
Fort Myers, FL
33901
(813) 334-3614

The Hemingway
Home
and Museum
907 Whitehead
Key West, FL 33040
(305) 294-1575

Historical Museum
of Southern Florida
101 W. Flagler St.
Miami, FL 33130
(305) 375-1492

Museum of Florida
History
500 S. Bronough St.
Tallahassee, FL
32399
(904) 488-1484

Museum of Science
& History
1025 Gulf Life Dr.
Jacksonville, FL
32207
(904) 396-7062

Pensacola
Historical Museum
405 S. Adams St.
Pensacola, FL 32501
(904) 433-1559

**St. Augustine Historical Society**
271 Charlotte St.
St. Augustine, FL 32084
(904) 824-2872

## Georgia

**Atlanta Historical Society**
3101 Andrews Drive, NW
Atlanta, GA 30305
(404) 261-1837

**The Columbus Museum**
1251 Wynnton Rd.
Columbus, GA 31906
(404) 322-0400

**DeKalb Historical Society Museum**
Old Courthouse on the Square
Decatur, GA 30030
(404) 373-2571

**Jekyll Island Museum**
Stable Rd.
Jekyll Island, GA 31520
(912) 635-2119

**William Scarbrough House**
41 West Broad St.
Savannah, GA 31402
(912) 233-7787

## Hawaii

**Bishop Museum**
1525 Bernice St.
Honolulu, HI 96817
(808) 847-3511

**Hulihee Palace**
75-5718 Alii Dr.
Kailua-Kona, HI 96740

**Iolani Palace**
King & Richards Sts.
Honolulu, HI 96813
(808) 522-0822

**Kauai Museum**
4428 Rice St.
Lihue, HI 96766
(808) 245-6931

**Lyman House Memorial Museum**
276 Haili St.
Hilo, HI 96720
(808) 935-5021

## Idaho

**Idaho State Historical Society**
610 N. Julia Davis Dr.
Boise, ID 83702
(208) 334-2120

**Museum of North Idaho**
115 NW Blvd.
Couer d'Alene, ID 83814
(208) 664-3448

## Illinois

**Chicago Architecture Foundation**
1800 S. Prairie Ave.
Chicago, IL 60616
(312) 326-1393

**Chicago Historical Society**
Clark St. at North Ave.
Chicago, IL 60614
(312) 642-4600

**Frankfort Area Historical Museum**
2000 E. St. Louis St.
West Frankfort, IL 62896
(618) 932-6159

**Lincoln Log Cabin State Historic Site**
R.R. 1
Lerna, IL 62440
(217) 345-6489

**Peoria Historical Society**
942 NE Glen Oak Ave.
Peoria, IL 61603
(309) 674-1921

**Frank Lloyd Wright Home and Studio**
951 Chicago Ave.
Oak Park, IL 60302
(708) 848-1976

University Museum
Southern Illinois
University
Carbondale, IL
62901
(618) 453-5388

## Indiana

Bartholomew
County Historical
Society
524 Third St.
Columbus, IN
47201
(812) 372-3541

Conner Prairie
13400 Allisonville
Rd.
Noblesville, IN
46060
(317) 776-6014

Historic Madison,
Inc.
500 West Street
Madison, IN 47250
(812) 265-2967

Historic New
Harmony
506 1/2 Main St.
New Harmony, IN
47631
(812) 682-4488

Indiana State
Museum
202 N. Alabama St.
Indianapolis, IN
46204
(317) 232-1637

President Benjamin
Harrison
Memorial Home
1230 N. Delaware
St.
Indianapolis, IN
46202
(317) 631-1898

Studebaker
National Museum
Century Center
120 S. St. Joseph St.
South Bend, IN
46601
(219) 284-9714

Tippecanoe County
Historical Museum
909 South St.
Lafayette, IN 47901
(317) 742-8411

Wayne County
Historical Museum
1150 North A St.
Richmond, IN
47374
(317) 962-5756

## Iowa

Cedar Falls
Historical Society
303 Clay St.
Cedar Falls, IA
50613
(319) 266-5149

Fort Dodge
Historical Museum
Museum Rd.
Fort Dodge, IA
50501
(515) 573-4231

Grout Museum
of History
and Science
503 South St.
Waterloo, IA 50701
(319) 234-6357

Iowa State
Historical Museum
600 E. Locust St.
Des Moines, IA
50319
(515) 281-5111

Jackson County
Historical Museum
Fairgrounds
Maquoketa, IA
52060
(319) 652-5020

## Kansas

Boot Hill Museum
Front St.
Dodge City, KS
67801
(316) 227-8188

Dickinson County
Historical Society
412 S. Campbell St.
Abilene, KS 67410
(913) 263-2681

**Fort Hays State
Museum**
Fort Hays State
University
600 Park St.
Hays, KS 67601
(913) 628-5664

**Pioneer Museum**
430 W. 4th St.
Ashland, KS 67831
(316) 635-2227

**Riley County
Historical Museum**
2309 Claflin Rd.
Manhattan, KS
66502
(913) 537-2210

**Smoky Hill
Museum**
211 W. Iron Ave.
Salina, KS 67401
(913) 827-3958

**Wichita-Sedgwick
County
Historical Museum**
204 S. Main
Wichita, KS 67202
(316) 265-9314

# Kentucky

**Farmington**
3033 Bardstown Rd.
Louisville, KY
40205
(502) 452-9920

**Kentucky Derby
Museum**
704 Central Ave.
Louisville, KY 40201
(502) 637-1111

**Kentucky
Historical Society**
Broadway at St.
Clair Mall
Frankfort, KY 40602
(502) 564-3016

**Kentucky Railway
Museum**
Ormsby Station Site
Lagrange Rd. &
Dorsey Ln.
Louisville, KY 40223
(502) 245-6035

**Museum of History
and Science**
727 Main St.
Louisville, KY 40202
(502) 561-6100

**National Museum
of the Boy Scouts
of America**
Murray State
University
Murray, KY 42071
(502) 762-3383

# Louisiana

**Acadian House
Museum**
1200 N. Main St.
St. Martinville, LA
70582
(318) 394-4284

**Emy-Lou
Biedenharn
Foundation**
2006 Riverside Dr.
Monroe, LA 71201
(318) 387-5281

**Gallier House**
1118 Royal St.
New Orleans, LA
70116
(504) 523-6722

**Hermann-Grima
House**
820 St. Louis St.
New Orleans, LA
70112
(504) 525-5661

**The Historic
New Orleans
Collection**
533 Royal St.
New Orleans, LA
70130
(504) 523-4662

**Longue Vue House
& Gardens**
7 Bamboo Rd.
New Orleans, LA
70124
(504) 488-5488

**Louisiana State
Museum**
751 Chartres St.
New Orleans, LA
70116
(504) 568-6968

**Magnolia Mound
Plantation**
2161 Nicholson Dr.
Baton Rouge, LA
70802
(504) 343-4955

**Pioneer Heritage
Center**
LSU Shreveport
8515 Youree Dr.
Shreveport, LA
71115
(318) 797-5332

**The Shadows-on-
the-Teche**
317 E. Main St.
New Iberia, LA
70560
(318) 369-6446

# Maine

**Brick Store
Museum**
117 Main St.
Kennebunk, ME
04043
(207) 985-4802

**Fort Western
Museum**
City Center Plaza
16 Cony St.
Augusta, ME 04330
(207) 626-2385

**Maine State
Museum**
State House
Complex
Augusta, ME 04333
(207) 289-2301

**United Society
of Shakers**
Sabbathday Lake
Poland Springs, ME
04274
(207) 926-4597

# Maryland

**Calvert Marine
Museum**
14200 Solomons
Island Rd.
Solomons, MD
20688
(301) 326-2042

**Historic Annapolis
Foundation**
194 Prince George St.
Annapolis, MD
21401
(301) 267-7619

**Historic
St. Mary's City**
Rt. #5
St. Mary's City, MD
20686
(301) 862-0990

**United States
Naval Academy
Museum**
Annapolis, MD
21402
(301) 267-2108

**Washington
County Historical
Society**
135 W. Washington St.
Hagerstown, MD
21740
(301) 797-8782

# Massachusetts

**Concord Museum**
200 Lexington Rd.
Concord, MA 01742
(508) 369-9763

**Danvers Historical
Society**
13 Page St.
Danvers, MA 01923
(508) 777-1666

**New Bedford
Whaling Museum**
18 Johnny Cake Hill
New Bedford, MA
02740
(508) 997-0046

**Old Sturbridge
Village**
1 Old Sturbridge
Village Rd.
Sturbridge, MA
01566
(508) 347-3362

Peabody Museum
of Salem
East India Square
Salem, MA 01970
(508) 745-1876

Plimoth Plantation
Warren Ave.
Plymouth, MA
02360
(508) 746-1622

The Paul Revere
House
19 North Square
Boston, MA 02113
(617) 523-2338

## Michigan

Jesse Besser
Museum
491 Johnson St.
Alpena, MI 49707
(517) 356-2202

Dearborn
Historical Museum
915 Brady St.
Dearborn, MI 48124
(313) 565-3000

Detroit Historical
Museum
5401 Woodward Ave.
Detroit, MI 48202
(313) 833-1805

Henry Ford
Museum
and Greenfield
Village
20900 Oakwood
Blvd.
Dearborn, MI 48121
(313) 271-1620

Iron County
Museum
Museum Lane
Caspian, MI 49915
(906) 265-3942

Kelsey Museum
of Ancient
& Mediaeval
Archaeology
434 S. State St.
Ann Arbor, MI
48109
(313) 764-9304

Mackinac State
Historical Parks
Fort Mackinac
and Mackinac
Island State Park
Mackinac Island,
MI 49757
(517) 373-4296

Marquette County
Historical Society
213 N. Front St.
Marquette, MI
49855
(906) 226-3571

Michigan
Historical Museum
717 W. Allegan St.
Lansing, MI 48918

Michigan State
University Museum
West Circle Drive
East Lansing, MI
48824
(517) 355-2370

Museum of Arts
and History
1115 Sixth St.
Port Huron, MI
48060
(313) 982-0891

## Minnesota

Blue Earth County
Historical Society
415 Cherry St.
Mankato, MN
56001
(507) 345-5566

A.M. Chisholm
Museum
506 W. Michigan St.
Duluth, MN 55802
(218) 722-8563

Minnesota
Historical Society
690 Cedar St.
St. Paul, MN 55101
(612) 296-2747

## Mississippi

Cairo Museum
Vicksburg National
Military Park
3201 Clay St.
Vicksburg, MS
39180
(601) 636-2199

Cottonlandia
Museum
Highway 82-49
Bypass
Greenwood, MS
38930
(601) 453-0925

Mississippi State
Historical Society
North State &
Capitol Sts.
Jackson, MS 39205
(601) 354-6222

## Missouri

Harry S. Truman
Museum
U.S. 24 & Delaware Sts.
Independence, MO
64050
(816) 833-1400

The Kansas City
Museum
3218 Gladstone
Blvd.
Kansas City, MO
64123
(816) 483-8300

Missouri Historical
Society
Lindel
& De Baliviere Sts.
St. Louis, MO 63112
(314) 361-1424

Museum
of Ozarks' History
603 E. Calhoun
Springfield, MO
65802
(417) 869-1976

Pony Express
Museum
914 Penn St.
St. Joseph, MO
64503
(816) 279-5059

## Montana

Copper King
Mansion
219 W. Granite
Butte, MT 59701
(406) 782-7580

Copper Village
Museum
401 E. Commercial
Anaconda, MT
59711
(406) 563-2422

Historical Museum
at Fort Missoula
Fort Missoula
Missoula, MT 59801
(406) 728-3476

Montana
Historical Society
225 N. Roberts
Helena, MT 59620
(406) 444-2694

Pioneer Museum
Highway #2 W.
Glasgow, MT 59230
(406) 228-2702

Western Heritage
Center
2822 Montana Ave.
Billings, MT 59101
(406) 256-6809

## Nebraska

Brownville
Historical
Society Museum
Main St.
Brownville, NE
68321
(402) 825-6001

Great Plains
Black Museum
2213 Lake St.
Omaha, NE 68110
(402) 345-2212

Hall of History
Boys Town, NE
68010
(402) 498-1185

Museum
of the Fur Trade
East Highway 20
Chadron, NE 69337
(308) 432-3843

**Stuhr Museum
of the Prairie
Pioneer**
3133 W. Highway 34
Grand Island, NE
68801
(308) 381-5316

**Western Heritage
Museum**
801 S. 10th St.
Omaha, NE 68108
(402) 444-5071

# Nevada

**Nevada Historical
Society**
1650 N. Virginia St.
Reno, NV 89503
(702) 789-0190

**The Nevada State
Museum**
600 N. Carson St.
Carson City, NV
89710
(702) 885-4810

# New
Hampshire

**Manchester
Historical
Association**
129 Amherst St.
Manchester, NH
03101
(603) 622-7531

**John Paul Jones
House**
43 Middle St.
Portsmouth, NH
03801
(603) 436-8420

**Strawbery Banke**
454 Court St.
Portsmouth, NH
03801
(603) 433-1100

# New Jersey

**Camden County
Historical Society**
Park Blvd.
& Euclid Ave.
Camden, NJ 08103
(609) 964-3333

**Cape May County
Historical Museum**
Route #9 - R.D.
Cape May Court
House, NJ
08210
(609) 465-3535

**The Thomas Clarke
House**
500 Mercer St.
Princeton, NJ 08540
(609) 921-0074

**Fosterfields Living
Historical Farm**
Kahdena Rd. &
Route #24
Morristown, NJ
07962
(201) 326-7645

**Historic Speedwell**
333 Speedwell Ave.
Morristown, NJ
07960
(201) 540-0211

# New Mexico

**Kit Carson
Foundation**
222 Ledoux St.
Taos, NM 87571
(505) 758-0505

**Museum
of New Mexico**
113 Lincoln Ave.
Santa Fe, NM 87504
(505) 827-6450

**The Wheelwright
Museum
of the American
Indian**
704 Camino Lejo
Santa Fe, NM 87502
(505) 982-4636

# New York

(Note: New York City
has a separate
section)

**Albany Institute
of History and Art**
125 Washington Ave.
Albany, NY 12210
(518) 463-4478

The Bronx County
Historical Society
3309 Bainbridge Ave.
Bronx, NY 10467
(212) 881-8900

David Conklin
Farmhouse
2 High St.
Huntington, NY
11743
(516) 427-7045

Erie Canal
Museum
318 Erie Blvd. E.
Syracuse, NY 13202
(315) 471-0593

Genesee County
Museum
Flint Hill Road
Mumford, NY 14511
(716) 538-6822

Geneva Historical
Society
and Museum
543 South Main St.
Geneva, NY 14456
(315) 789-5151

Madison County
Historical
Society - Cottage
Lawn
435 Main St.
Oneida, NY 13421
(315) 363-4136

National Baseball
Hall of Fame
and Museum
Main Street
Cooperstown, NY
13326

New York State
Museum
Empire State Plaza
Albany, NY 12230
(518) 474-5877

Richardson-Bates
House Museum
135 E. 3rd St.
Oswego, NY 13126
(315) 343-1342

Sagamore Hill
National Historic
Site
20 Sagamore Hill Rd.
Oyster Bay, NY
11771
(516) 922-4447

Vanderbilt
Museum: Mansion,
Marine Museum,
Planetarium
180 Little Neck Rd.
Centerport, NY
11721
(516) 262-7880

West Point
Museum,
United States
Military Academy
Bldg. 2110
West Point, NY
10996
(914) 938-2203

## New York City

The Jewish
Museum
1109 Fifth Ave.
New York, NY 10128
(212) 860-1888

Museum
of the American
Indian
Broadway at 155th St.
New York, NY 10032
(212) 283-2420

Statue of Liberty
National
Monument
Liberty Island
New York, NY 10004
(212) 363-3267

## North Carolina

Biltmore Estate
One North Pack
Square
Asheville, NC 28801
(704) 255-1776

Greensboro
Historical Museum
130 Summit Ave.
Greensboro, NC
27401
(919) 373-2043

North Carolina
Maritime Museum
315 Front St.
Beaufort, NC 28516
(919) 728-7317

North Carolina
Museum
of History
109 E. Jones St.
Raleigh, NC 27611
(919) 733-3894

Old Salem
600 S. Main St.
Winston-Salem, NC
27101
(919) 721-7300

Reynolda House
Reynolda Rd.
Winston-Salem, NC
27106
(919) 725-5325

# North Dakota

Frontier Museum
Williston, ND
58801
(701) 572-5006

Myra Museum
and Campbell
House
2405 Belmont Rd.
Grand Forks, ND
58201
(701) 775-2216

Red River
& Northern Plains
Regional Museum
West Fargo, ND
58078
(701) 282-2822

State Historical
Society of North
Dakota
North Dakota
Heritage Center
Bismarck, ND
58505
(701) 224-2666

# Ohio

McKinley Museum
of History, Science,
& Industry
800 McKinley
Monument Dr. NW
Canton, OH 44708
(216) 455-7043

Ohio Historical
Center
Interstate 71 & 17th
Ave.
Columbus, OH
43211
(614) 297-2300

Western Reserve
Historical Society
10825 East Blvd.
Cleveland, OH
44106
(216) 721-5722

U.S. Air Force
Museum, Wright-
Patterson AFB
Ohio 45433
(513) 255-3284

# Oklahoma

Museum
of the Great Plains
601 Ferris Ave.
Lawson, OK 73502
(405) 353-5675

National Cowboy
Hall of Fame
and Western
Heritage Center
1700 NE 63rd St.
Oklahoma City, OK
73111
(405) 478-2250

Oklahoma
Historical Society
2100 N. Lincoln Blvd.
Oklahoma City, OK
73105
(405) 521-2491

The Norman
Cleveland County
Historical Museum
508 N. Peters
Norman, OK 73070
(405) 321-0156

## Oregon

**American Advertising Museum**
9 NW Second Ave.
Portland, OR 97209
(503) 226-0000

**Mission Mill Museum**
1313 Mill St. SE
Salem, OR 97301
(503) 585-7012

**Oregon Historical Society**
1230 SW Park Ave.
Portland, OR 97205
(503) 222-1741

**Southern Oregon Historical Society**
206 N. 5th St.
Jacksonville, OR 97530
(503) 899-1847

## Pennsylvania

**Fort Hunter Mansion**
5300 N. Front St.
Harrisburg, PA 17110
(717) 599-5822

**Gettysburg National Military Park**
Gettysburg, PA 17325
(717) 334-1124

**Historic Bethlehem**
459 Old York Rd.
Bethlehem, PA 18018
(215) 691-5300

**Landis Valley Museum**
2451 Kissel Hill Rd.
Lancaster, PA 17601
(717) 569-0401

**Lehigh County Historical Society**
Hamilton at Fifth St.
Allentown, PA 18105
(215) 435-4664

**Philadelphia Maritime Museum**
321 Chestnut St.
Philadelphia, PA
(215) 925-5439

**State Museum of Pennsylvania**
3rd and North Sts.
Harrisburg, PA 17120
(717) 787-4980

**Washington Crossing Historic Park**
Washington Crossing, PA 18977
(215) 493-4076

## Rhode Island

**The Preservation Society of Newport County**
118 Mill St.
Newport, RI 02840
(401) 847-1000

**Rhode Island Historical Society**
110 Benevolent St.
Providence, RI 02906
(401) 331-8575

## South Carolina

**The Charleston Museum**
360 Meeting St.
Charleston, SC 29403
(803) 722-2996

**Drayton Hall**
3380 Ashley River Rd.
Charleston, SC 29414
(803) 766-0188

**Fort Sumter National Monument**
1214 Middle St.
Sullivan's Island, SC 29482
(803) 883-3123

Hampton-Preston
Mansion
and Garden
1615 Blanding St.
Columbia, SC 29201
(803) 252-3964

Museum
of African-
American Culture
1403 Richland St.
Columbia, SC 29201
(803) 252-1450

South Carolina
State Museum
301 Gervais St.
Columbia, SC 29201
(803) 737-4921

John Mark Verdier
House
801 Bay St.
Beaufort, SC 29902
(803) 524-6334

## South Dakota

Siouxland
Heritage Museum
200 W. 6th St.
Sioux Falls, SD
57102
(605) 335-4210

South Dakota State
Historical Society
900 Governors Dr.
Pierre, SD 57501
(605) 773-3458

## Tennessee

Belle Meade
Mansion
110 Leake Ave.
Nashville, TN 37205
(615) 356-0501

Blount Mansion
200 W. Hill Ave.
Knoxville, TN
37902
(615) 525-2375

Chattanooga
Regional History
Museum
201 High St.
Chattanooga, TN
37403
(615) 265-3247

Clarksville-
Montgomery
County Historical
Museum
100 S. Second St.
Clarksville, TN
37040
(615) 648-5780

Historic Rugby
State Highway 52
Rugby, TN 37733
(615) 628-2441

Museum
of Appalachia
Norris, TN 37828
(615) 494-7680

Ramsey House
2614 Thorngrove
Pike
Knoxville, TN
37914
(615) 546-0745

Tennessee
State Museum
505 Deaderick St.
Nashville, TN 37219
(615) 741-2692

## Texas

The Alamo
Alamo Plaza
San Antonio, TX
78299
(512) 222-1693

Caddo Indian
Museum
701 Hardy St.
Longview, TX 75604
(214) 759-5739

Fort Worth
Museum of Science
and History
1501 Montgomery St.
Fort Worth, TX
76107
(817) 732-7635

Galveston
Historical Museum
2219 Market St.
Galveston, TX
77550
(409) 766-2340

**Institute of Texan Cultures**
801 S. Bowie at Durango Blvd.
San Antonio, TX 78205
(512) 226-7651

**Museum of the Southwest**
1705 W. Missouri Ave.
Midland, TX 79701
(915) 683-2882

**Panhandle-Plains Historical Museum**
2401 Fourth Ave.
Canyon, TX 79016
(806) 656-2244

# Utah

**Ogden Union Station Museums**
25th & Wall Ave.
Ogden, UT 84401
(801) 629-8444

**Utah State Historical Society**
300 Rio Grande St.
Salt Lake City, UT 84101
(801) 533-5755

# Vermont

**Billings Farm & Museum**
River Rd. & Rt. 12
Woodstock, VT 05091
(802) 457-2355

**Hildene**
Route 7A
Manchester, VT 05254
(802) 362-1788

**Vermont Museum**
109 State St.
Montpelier, VT 05602
(802) 828-2291

# Virginia

**Arlington House, Arlington National Cemetary**
Arlington, VA 22211
(703) 557-0613

**Carlyle House Historic Park**
121 N. Fairfax St.
Alexandria, VA 22314
(703) 549-2997

**Colonial Williamsburg**
Williamsburg, VA 23815
(804) 229-1000

**Gunston Hall**
10709 Gunston Rd.
Mason Neck, VA 22079
(703) 550-9220

**Stonewall Jackson House**
8 E. Washington St.
Lexington, VA 24450
(703) 463-2552

**Jamestown Museum**
Jamestown Island
Jamestown, VA 23081
(804) 898-3400

**The Mariners' Museum**
100 Museum Dr.
Newport News, VA 23606
(804) 595-0368

**Monticello**
Charlottesville, VA 22902
(804) 293-2158

**Mount Vernon**
George Washington Pkwy. So.
Mount Vernon, VA 22121
(703) 780-2000

The Museum
of the Confederacy
1201 E. Clay St.
Richmond, VA
23219
(804) 649-1861

Museum
of American
Frontier Culture
Richmond Road
Stauton, VA 24401
(703) 332-7850

Roanoke Valley
Historical Museum
One Market Square
Roanoke, VA 24011
(703) 342-5770

Sherwood Forest
Plantation
Route #5
Charles City, VA
23020
(804) 829-5377

Shirley Plantation
501 Shirley
Plantation Rd.
Charles City, VA
23030
(804) 795-2385

Smithfield
Plantation
Southgate Dr.
Extension
Blacksburg, VA
24060
(703) 951-2060

Woodlawn
Plantation
9000 Richmond
Highway
Alexandria, VA
22309
(703) 780-4000

# Washington

Cheney Cowles
Museum
W. 2316 First Ave.
Spokane, WA 99204
(509) 456-3931

Clark County
Historical Museum
1511 Main St.
Vancouver, WA
98663
(206) 695-4681

Fort Walla Walla
Museum Complex
Myra Road
Walla Walla, WA
99362
(509) 525-7703

Museum of History
and Industry
2700 24th Ave. East
Seattle, WA 98112
(206) 324-1125

Pioneer Farm
Museum
7716 Ohop Valley Rd.
Eatonville, WA
98328
(206) 832-6300

San Juan
Historical Society
405 Price St.
Friday Harbor, WA
98250
(206) 378-3949

Washington
State Capital
Museum
211 W. 21st Ave.
Olympia, WA
98501
(206) 753-2580

Whatcom Museum
of History and Art
121 Prospect St.
Bellingham, WA
98225
(206) 676-6981

Yakima Nation
Museum
Highway 97 & Fort
Rd.
Toppenish, WA
98948
(509) 865-2800

Yakima Valley
Museum
2105 Tieton Dr.
Yakima, WA 98902
(509) 248-0747

# West Virginia

Harpers Ferry
Center
Harpers Ferry, WV
24525
(304) 535-6371

Oglebay Institute
Mansion Museum
Oglebay Park
Wheeling, WV
26003
(304) 242-7272

West Virginia
State Museum
Capitol Complex
Charleston, WV
25305
(304) 348-0230

## Wisconsin

Chippewa Valley
Museum
Carson Park
Eau Claire, WI
54703
(715) 834-7871

Fairlawn Mansion
& Museum
906 E. 2nd St.
Superior, WI 54880
(715) 394-5712

Galloway House
and Village
336 Old Pioneer Rd.
Fond du Lac, WI
54935
(414) 922-6390

Hixon House
429 N. 7th St.
La Crosse, WI 54601
(608) 782-1980

Manitowoc
Maritime Museum
75 Maritime Dr.
Manitowoc, WI
54220
(414) 684-0218

Milwaukee County
Historical Society
910 N. Old World
Third St.
Milwaukee, WI
53203
(414) 273-8288

## Wyoming

Buffalo Bill
Historical Center
720 Sheridan Ave.
Cody, WY 82414
(307) 587-4771

Fort Casper
Museum
4001 Fort Caspar Rd.
Casper, WY 82601
(307) 235-8462

Laramie Plains
Museum
603 Ivinson
Laramie, WY 82070
(307) 742-4448

Wyoming State
Museum
24th & Central Ave.
Cheyenne, WY
82002
(307) 777-7022

# Science Museums

## Alabama

**Birmingham Zoo**
2630 Cahaba Rd.
Birmingham, AL
35223
(205) 879-0409

**The Discovery
Place
of Birmingham,
Inc.**
1320 22nd St. South
Birmingham, AL
35205
(205) 939-1176

**Exploreum**
1906 Springhill Ave.
Mobile, AL 36607
(205) 471-5923

## Alaska

**Alaska State
Museum**
395 Whittier
Juneau, AK 99801
(907) 465-2901

**University
of Alaska Museum**
907 Yukon Dr.
Fairbanks, AK
99775
(907) 474-7505

## Arizona

**Arizona Museum
of Science &
Technology**
80 N. Second St.
Phoenix, AZ 85004
(602) 256-9388

**Arizona-Sonora
Desert Museum**
2021 N. Kinney Rd.
Tucson, AZ 85743
(602) 883-1380

Arizona Zoological
Society
5810 E. Van Buren
Phoenix, AZ 85072
(602) 273-1341

**Museum
of Northern
Arizona**
Fort Valley Rd.
Flagstaff, AZ 86001
(602) 774-5211

## Arkansas

**Arkansas Museum
of Science
and History**
MacArthur Park
Little Rock, AR
72202
(501) 371-3521

Hot Springs
National Park
369 Central Ave.
Bathhouse Row
Hot Springs, AR
71901
(501) 624-3383

Little Rock
Zoological Gardens
1 Jonesboro Dr.
Little Rock, AR
72205
(501) 666-2406

## California

**California
Academy
of Sciences**
Golden Gate Park
San Francisco, CA
94118
(415) 221-5100

California Museum
of Science and
Industry
700 State Dr.
Los Angeles, CA
90037
(213) 744-7400

**Exploratorium**
Marina Blvd.
& Lyon St.
San Francisco, CA
94133
(415) 561-0360

**Fowler Museum
of Cultural History**
University of
California
Los Angeles, CA
90024
(213) 825-4361

**Lawrence Hall
of Science**
University
of California
Centennial Drive
Berkeley, CA 94720
(415) 642-5133

**Los Angeles
Children's Museum**
310 North Main St.
Los Angeles, CA
90012
(213) 687-8801

**The Museum
of Natural History
and Science**
2627 Vista del Oro
Newport Beach, CA
92660
(714) 640-7120

**National
Maritime Museum**
Hyde Street Pier
San Francisco, CA
94109
(415) 556-3002

**Natural History
Museum
of Los Angeles
County**
900 Exposition
Blvd.
Los Angeles, CA
90007
(213) 744-3414

**The Oakland
Museum**
1000 Oak St.
Oakland, CA 94607
(415) 273-3401

**Palm Springs
Desert Museum**
101 Museum Drive
Palm Springs, CA
92262
(619) 325-7186

**Redwood
National Park**
1111 2nd St.
Crescent City, CA
95531
(707) 464-6101

**Sacramento
Science
and Junior
Museum**
3615 Auburn Blvd.
Sacramento, CA
95821
(916) 449-8255

**San Diego Natural
History Museum**
Balboa Park
San Diego, CA
92101
(619) 232-3821

**San Diego Zoo**
San Diego, CA
92112
(619) 231-1515

**Santa Barbara
Museum
of Natural History**
2559 Puesta del Sol
Rd.
Santa Barbara, CA
93105
(805) 682-4711

**The Yosemite
Museum, National
Park Service**
Yosemite National
Park, CA
(209) 372-0281

## Colorado

Cheyenne
Mountain
Zoological Park
4250 Cheyenne Mt.
Zoo Rd.
Colorado Springs,
CO 80906
(719) 633-9925

Denver Museum
of Natural History
City Park
Denver, CO 80205
(303) 370-6357

Museum
of Western
Colorado
248 S. 4th St.
Grand Junction, CO
81501
(303) 242-0971

University
of Colorado
Museum
Broadway, between
15th & 16th Sts.
Boulder, CO 80309
(719) 492-6165

Western Museum
of Mining
and Industry
1025 North Gate Rd.
Colorado Springs,
CO 80921
(719) 598-8850

## Connecticut

The Bruce Museum
Museum Drive
Greenwich, CT
06830
(203) 869-0376

Museum of Art,
Science
and Industry
4450 Park Ave.
Bridgeport, CT
06604
(203) 372-3521

Peabody Museum
of Natural History
Yale University
170 Whitney Ave.
New Haven, CT
06511
(203) 432-3750

Science Museum
of Connecticut
950 Trout Brook Dr.
West Hartford, CT
06119
(203) 236-2961

Thames Science
Center
Gallows Lane
New London, CT
06320
(203) 442-0391

## Delaware

Delaware
Agricultural
Museum
866 N. Dupont
Hwy.
Dover, DE 19901
(302) 734-1618

Delaware Museum
of Natural History
4840 Kennett Pike
Wilmington, DE
19807
(302) 658-9111

## District
## of Columbia

National
Zoological Park
3000 Connecticut
Ave., NW
Washington, DC
20008
(202) 673-4800

Smithsonian
Institution
(collection of
history, science, art,
and air/space
museums)
1000 Jefferson Dr.
Washington, DC
20560
(202) 357-1300

## Florida

**Edison Winter Home and Museum**
2350 McGregor Blvd.
Fort Myers, FL 33901
(813) 334-3614

**Everglades National Park**
Homestead, FL 33030
(305) 247-6211

**Florida Museum of Natural History**
University of Florida
Gainesville, FL 32611
(904) 392-1721

**Metrozoo**
12400 SW 152nd St.
Miami, FL 33177
(305) 251-0401

**Museum of Arts and Sciences**
1040 Museum Blvd.
Daytona Beach, FL 32014
(904) 255-0285

**Museum of Science**
3280 S. Miami Ave.
Miami, FL 33129
(305) 854-4247

**Museum of Science & History**
1025 Gulf Life Dr.
Jacksonville, FL 32207
(904) 396-7062

**Museum of Science and Industry**
4801 E. Fowler Ave.
Tampa, FL 33617
(813) 985-5531

**Orlando Science Center**
Loch Haven Park
810 E. Rollins Ave.
Orlando, FL 32803
(305) 896-7151

**Science Center of Pinellas County**
7701 22nd Ave.N.
St. Petersburg, FL 33710
(813) 384-0027

## Georgia

**Fernbank Science Center**
156 Heaton Park Dr., NE
Atlanta, GA 30307
(404) 378-4311

**Museum of Arts and Sciences**
4182 Forsyth Rd.
Macon, GA 31210
(912) 477-3232

**Savannah Science Museum**
4405 Paulsen St.
Savannah, GA 31405
(912) 355-6705

**Telfair Academy of Arts and Sciences**
121 Bernard St.
Savannah, GA 31401
(912) 232-1177

**Zoo Atlanta**
800 Cherokee Ave., SE
Atlanta, GA 30315
(404) 624-5600

## Hawaii

**Bishop Museum**
1525 Bernice St.
Honolulu, HI 96817
(808) 847-3511

**Honolulu Zoo**
151 Kapahulu Ave.
Honolulu, HI 96815
(808) 923-4772

**Lyman House Memorial Museum**
276 Haili St.
Hilo, HI 96720
(808) 935-5021

## Idaho

Idaho Museum
of Natural History
Idaho State
University
Pocatello, ID 83209
(208) 236-3168

## Illinois

Burpee Museum
of Natural History
813 N. Main St.
Rockford, IL 61103
(815) 965-3132

Chicago
Architecture
Foundation
1800 S. Prarie Ave.
Chicago, IL 60616
(312) 326-1393

Chicago Zoological
Park
(Brookfield Zoo)
8400 W. 31st St.
Brookfield, IL 60513
(708) 485-0263

Field Museum
of Natural History
Roosevelt Rd. at
Lake Shore Dr.
Chicago, IL 60605
(312) 922-9410

Illinois State
Museum
Spring & Edwards Sts.
Springfield, IL
62706
(217) 782-7386

Lakeview Museum
of Arts
and Sciences
1125 West Lake Ave.
Peoria, IL 61614
(309) 686-7000

Lincoln Park Zoo
2200 N. Cannon Dr.
Chicago, IL 60614
(312) 935-2249

Museum of Science
and Industry
57th & Lake Shore
Dr.
Chicago, IL 60637
(312) 684-1414

Quincy Museum
of Natural History
and Art
1601 Maine St.
Quincy, IL 62301
(217) 224-7669

University Museum
Southern Illinois
University
Carbondale, IL
62901
(618) 453-5388

## Indiana

The Chidren's
Museum
3000 N. Meridian St.
Indianapolis, IN
46208
(317) 921-4019

Evansville Museum
of Arts & Science
411 SE Riverside Dr.
Evansville, IN 47713
(812) 425-2406

Indianapolis Zoo
1200 W.
Washington St.
Indianapolis, IN
46218
(317) 638-8072

## Iowa

Grout Museum
of History
and Science
503 South St.
Waterloo, IA 50701
(319) 234-6357

Putnam Museum
1717 W. Twelfth St.
Davenport, IA
52804
(319) 324-1933

Sanford Museum
and Planetarium
117 E. Willow St.
Cherokee, IA 51012
(712) 225-3922

## Kansas

Museum
of Natural History
University of Kansas
Lawrence, KS 66045
(913) 864-4540

## Kentucky

Behringer-
Crawford Museum
1600 Montague Rd.
Devou Park
Covington, KY
41012
(606) 491-4003

International
Museum
of the Horse
4089 Iron Works Pike
Lexington, KY
40511
(606) 233-4303

Kentucky Railway
Museum
Ormsby Station
Site
Lagrange Rd.
& Dorsey Ln.
Louisville, KY 40223
(502) 245-6035

The Living Arts
and Science Center
362 N. Martin
Luther King Blvd.
Lexington, KY
40508
(606) 252-5222

Museum
of Anthropology
Northern Kentucky
University
University Drive
Highland Heights,
KY 41076
(606) 572-5259

Museum of History
and Science
727 Main St.
Louisville, KY 40202
(502) 561-6100

## Louisiana

Audubon Park
& Zoological
Garden
6500 Magazine St.
New Orleans, LA
70178
(504) 861-2537

Children's Museum
of Lake Charles
809 Kirby St.
Lake Charles, LA
70601
(318) 433-9420

Lafayette Natural
History Museum
637 Girard Dr.
Lafayette, LA 70503
(318) 268-5544

Louisiana
Arts and Science
Center
100 S. River Rd.
Baton Rouge, LA
70801
(504) 344-9463

Louisiana Nature
& Science Center
Joe Brown Memorial
Park
New Orleans, LA
70127
(504) 246-5672

## Maine

Maine State
Museum
State House
Complex
Augusta, ME 04333
(207) 289-2301

The Natural
History Museum
College of the
Atlantic
Bar Harbor, ME
04609
(207) 288-5015

## Maryland

Baltimore Museum
of Industry
1415 Key Highway
Baltimore, MD
21230
(301) 727-4808

Calvert Marine
Museum
14200 Solomons
Island Rd.
Solomons, MD
20688

Maryland Science
Center
601 Light St.
Baltimore, MD
21217
(301) 685-5225

National
Aquarium
in Baltimore
501 E. Pratt St.
Baltimore, MD
21202
(301) 576-3800

## Massachusetts

The Berkshire
Museum
39 South St.
Pittsfield, MA 01201
(413) 443-7171

Cape Cod Museum
of Natural History
Rt. #6A
Brewster, MA 02631

Children's Museum
Museum Wharf
300 Congress St.
Boston, MA 02210
(617) 426-6500

The Computer
Museum
300 Congress St.
Boston, MA 02210
(617) 426-2800

The Discovery
Museums
177 Main St.
Acton, MA 01720
(508) 264-4200

New England
Science Center
222 Harington Way
Worchester, MA
01604

The MIT Museum
265 Massachusetts
Ave.
Cambridge, MA
02139
(617) 253-4429

Museum of Science
Science Park
Boston, MA 02114
(617) 589-0100

## Michigan

Ann Arbor
Hands-On Museum
219 E. Huron St.
Ann Arbor, MI
48104
(313) 995-5437

Jesse Besser
Museum
491 Johnson St.
Alpena, MI 49707
(517) 356-2202

Chippewa Nature
Center
400 S. Badour Rd.
Midland, MI 48640
(517) 631-0830

Detroit Science
Center
5020 John R. St.
Detroit, MI 48202
(313) 577-8400

Great Lakes Area
Paleontological
Museum
381 S. Long Lake Rd.
Traverse City, MI
49684
(616) 943-8850

Impressions 5
Science Museum
200 Museum Dr.
Lansing, MI 48933
(517) 485-8116

Kalamazoo
Nature Center
7000 N. Westnedge
Ave.
Kalamazoo, MI
49007
(616) 381-1574

Michigan State
University
Museum
West Circle Drive
East Lansing, MI
48824
(517) 355-2370

University of
Michigan
Museum of
Zoology
1109 Washtenaw
Ann Arbor, MI
48109
(313) 764-0476

## Minnesota

James Ford Bell
Museum
of Natural History
10 Church St., S.E.
Minneapolis, MN
55455
(612) 624-1852

A.M. Chisholm
Museum
506 W. Michigan St.
Duluth, MN 55802

Lake Superior
Museum
of Transportation
506 W. Michigan St.
Duluth, MN 55802
(218) 727-0687

The Science
Museum
of Minnesota
30 E. 10th St.
St. Paul, MN 55101
(612) 221-9488

## Mississippi

John Martin
Frazier Museum
of Natural Science
University of
Southern Mississippi
East Memorial Drive
Hattiesburg, MS
39406

University
Museums
The University of
Mississippi
University, MS
38677
(601) 232-7073

## Missouri

National Museum
of Transportation
3015 Barrett Station
Rd.
St. Louis, MO 63122
(314) 965-6885

The Kansas City
Museum
3218 Gladstone Blvd.
Kansas City, MO
64123
(816) 483-8300

St. Louis
Science Center
Forest Park
St. Louis, MO 63110
(314) 289-4400

St. Louis
Zoological Park
Forest Park
St. Louis, MO 63110
(314) 781-0900

## Montana

Museum
of the Rockies
Montana State
University
Bozeman, MT
59717
(406) 994-2251

## Nebraska

Folsom Chidrens'
Zoo
and Botanical
Garden
2800 A St.
Lincoln, NE 68502
(402) 475-6741

Omaha Children's
Museum
551 S. 18th St.
Omaha, NE 68102
(402) 342-6164

University
of Nebraska
State Museum
307 Morrill Hall
14th & U Sts.
Lincoln, NE 68588
(402) 472-3779

## Nevada

Museum
of Natural History
University
of Nevada
4505 S. Marilyn
Parkway
Las Vegas, NV
89154
(702) 739-3381

The Nevada State
Museum
600 N. Carson St.
Carson City, NV
89710
(702) 885-4810

## New Hampshire

Audubon Society
of New Hampshire
3 Silk Farm Rd.
Concord, NH 03301
(603) 224-9909

## New Jersey

Bergen Museum
of Art & Science
Ridgewood &
Farview Aves.
Paramus, NJ 07652
(201) 265-1248

The Newark
Museum
49 Washington St.
Newark, NJ 07101
(201) 596-6550

New Jersey State
Museum
205 W. State St.
Trenton, NJ 08625

## New Mexico

Bradbury Science
Museum
Diamond Dr.
Los Alamos, NM
87545
(505) 667-4444

Carlsbad Caverns
National Park
3225 National Parks
Hwy.
Carlsbad, NM
88220
(505) 785-2232

Maxwell Museum
of Anthropology
University & Ash, NE
Albuquerque, NM
87131
(505) 277-4404

New Mexico
Museum
of Natural History
1801 Mountain Rd.
NW
Albuquerque, NM
87104
(505) 841-8837

The Space Center
Hwy. 2001
Alamagordo, NM
88310
(505) 437-2840

## New York

American Museum
of Natural History
Central Park West
at 79th St.
New York, NY 10024
(212) 769-5000

American Museum
- Hayden
Planetarium
81st & Central Park
West
New York, NY 10024
(212) 769-5900

The Brooklyn
Children's Museum
145 Brooklyn Ave.
Brooklyn, NY 11213
(718) 735-4400

Buffalo Museum
of Science
1020 Humbolt Pkwy.
Buffalo, NY 14211
(716) 896-5200

International
Museum
of Photography
George Eastman
House
900 East Ave.
Rochester, NY
14607
(716) 271-3361

New York State
Museum
Empire State Plaza
Albany, NY 12230
(518) 474-5877

Roberson Center
for the Arts
and Sciences
30 Front St.
Binghamton, NY
13905
(607) 772-0660

Rochester Museum
and Science Center
657 East Ave.
Rochester, NY
14603
(716) 271-4320

Schenectady
Museum
and Planetarium
Nott Terrace
Heights
Schenectady, NY
12308
(518) 382-7890

Sci-Tech Center
of Northern New
York
317 Washington St.
Watertown, NY
13601
(315) 788-1340

Staten Island
Institute
of Arts
and Sciences
75 Stuyvesant Place
Staten Island, NY
10301
(718) 727-1135

Vanderbilt
Museum: Mansion,
Marine Museum,
Planetarium
180 Little Neck Rd.
Centerport, NY
11721
(516) 262-7880

# North
# Carolina

Discovery Place
301 N. Tryon St.
Charlotte, NC
28202
(704) 372-6262

The Health
Adventure
501 Biltmore Ave.
Asheville, NC 28801
(704) 254-6373

Museum
of Anthropology
Wake Forest Dr.
Winston-Salem, NC
27109
(919) 761-5282

The Natural
Science Center
of Greensboro
4301 Lawndale Dr.
Greensboro, NC
27408
(919) 288-3769

Nature Museum
1658 Sterling Rd.
Charlotte, NC
28209
(704) 372-6261

North Carolina
Museum
of Life and Science
433 Murray Ave.
Durham, NC 27704
(919) 477-0431

Schiele Museum
of Natural History
and Planetarium
1500 E. Garrison
Blvd.
Gastonia, NC 28053
(704) 866-6900

Science Museums
of Charlotte
301 Tryon St.
Charlotte, NC
28202
(704) 372-6261

## North Dakota

**Dakota Zoo**
Sertona Park Rd.
Bismark, ND 58502
(701) 223-7543

## Ohio

**Center of Science and Industry**
280 E. Broad St.
Columbus, OH 43215
(614) 228-5619

**Cincinnati Museum of Natural History & Planetarium**
1720 Gilbert Ave.
Cincinnati, OH 45202
(513) 621-3889

**Cleveland Children's Museum**
10730 Euclid Ave.
Cleveland, OH 44106
(216) 791-7114

**Cleveland Museum of Natural History**
Wade Oval,
University Circle
Cleveland, OH 44106
(216) 231-4600

**Dayton Museum of Natural History**
2629 Ridge Ave.
Dayton, OH 45414
(513) 275-7431

**McKinley Museum of History, Science, & Industry**
800 McKinley Monument Dr. NW
Canton, OH 44708
(216) 455-7043

**Toledo Museum of Natural Sciences**
2700 Broadway
Toledo, OH 43609
(419) 385-5721

## Oklahoma

**Oklahoma Museum of Natural History**
University of Oklahoma
1335 Asp Ave.
Norman, OK 73019
(405) 325-4711

**Omniplex**
2100 NE 52 St.
Oklahoma City, OK 78111
(405) 424-5545

**Tulsa Zoological Park**
5701 E. 36th St. N.
Tulsa, OK 74115
(918) 596-2400

## Oregon

**The High Desert Museum**
59800 S. Hwy. 97
Bend, OR 97702
(503) 382-4754

**Oregon Museum of Science and Industry**
4015 SW Canyon Rd.
Portland, OR 97221
(503) 222-2828

**Willamette Science & Technology Center**
2300 Centennial Blvd.
Eugene, OR 97401
(503) 484-9027

## Pennsylvania

**Academy of Natural Sciences**
19th & the Parkway
Philadelphia, PA 19103
(215) 299-1000

**The Carnegie Museum of Natural History**
4400 Forbes Ave.
Pittsburgh, PA 15213
(412) 622-3243

Franklin Institute
Science Museum
and Planetarium
20th & the Parkway
Philadelphia, PA
19103
(215) 448-1200

The Frost
Entomological
Museum
The Pennsylvania
State University
University Park, PA
16802
(814) 863-1863

Pittsburgh
Children's Museum
Old Post Office -
Allegheny Center
Pittsburgh, PA
15212
(412) 322-5059

# Rhode Island

Haffenreffer
Museum
of Anthropology
Brown University
Mt. Hope Grant
Bristol, RI 02809
(401) 253-8388

# South Carolina

The Charleston
Museum
360 Meeting St.
Charleston, SC
29403
(803) 722-2996

Roper Mountain
Science Center
504 Roper
Mountain Rd.
Greenville, SC
29615
(803) 297-0232

# Tennessee

American Museum
of Science
and Energy
300 S. Tulane Ave.
Oak Ridge, TN
37830
(615) 576-3200

Children's Museum
of Oak Ridge
461 W. Outer Dr.
Oak Ridge, TN
37830
(615) 482-1074

Cumberland
Science Museum
800 Ridley Blvd.
Nashville, TN 37203
(615) 259-6099

Memphis Pink
Palace Museum
& Planetarium
3050 Central Ave.
Memphis, TN 38111
(901) 454-5600

# Texas

Dallas Museum
of Natural History
Fair Park
Dallas, TX 75210
(214) 670-8460

Fort Worth
Museum
of Science
and History
1501 Montgomery St.
Fort Worth, TX
76107
(817) 732-7635

Houston Museum
of Natural Science
1 Hermann Circle Dr.
Houston, TX 77030
(713) 639-4635

Insights-El Paso
Science Center
303 Oregon St.
El Paso, TX 79901
(915) 542-2990

The Petroleum
Museum
1500 Interstate 20 W.
Midland, TX 79701
(915) 683-4403

Southwest Museum
of Science
and Technology
Fair Park
Dallas, TX 75210
(214) 428-7200

Texas Memorial
Museum
2400 Trinity
Austin, TX 78705
(512) 471-1604

Wichita Falls
Museum
Two Eureka Circle
Wichita Falls, TX
76308
(817) 692-0923

Witte Museum
3801 Broadway
San Antonio,TX
78209
(512) 226-5544

## Utah

Children's
Museum of Utah
840 West
Salt Lake City, UT
84103
(801) 328-3383

Hansen
Planetarium
15 S. State St.
Salt Lake City, UT
84111
(801) 538-2104

Utah Museum
of Natural History
University of Utah
Salt Lake City, UT
84112
(801) 581-6927

## Vermont

Fairbanks Museum
and Planetarium
Main & Prospect Sts.
St. Johnsbury, VT
05819
(802) 748-2372

Montshire Museum
of Science
Montshire Rd.
Norwich, VT 05055
(802) 649-2200

## Virginia

The NASA Langley
Visitor Center
Langley Research
Center
Hampton, VA
23665
(804) 864-6000

Science Museum
of Virginia
2500 W. Broad St.
Richmond, VA
23220
(804) 367-6799

Science Museum
of Western
Virginia
1 Market Square
Roanoke, VA 24011
(703) 342-5710

Virginia Living
Museum
524 J. Clyde Morris
Blvd.
Newport News, VA
23601
(804) 595-1900

Virginia Marine
Science Museum
717 General Booth
Blvd.
Virginia Beach, VA
23451
(804) 425-3447

Virginia Museum
of Natural History
1001 Douglas Ave.
Martinsville, VA
24112
(703) 666-8600

## Washington

Museum of Flight
9404 E. Marginal
Way So.
Seattle, WA 98108
(206) 764-5700

Museum of History
and Industry
2700 24th Ave. East
Seattle, WA 98112
(206) 324-1125

Pacific Science
Center
200 2nd Ave. N.
Seattle, WA 98109
(206) 443-2001

Woodland Park
Zoological Garden
5500 Phinney Ave. N.
Seattle, WA 98103
(206) 684-4820

## West Virginia

Sunrise
Museums, Inc.
746 Myrtle Rd.
Charleston, WV
25314
(304) 344-8035

## Wisconsin

Logan Museum
of Anthropology
Beloit College
Beloit, WI 53511
(608) 365-3391

Madison
Children's Museum
100 State St.
Madison, WI 53703
(608) 256-6445

Milwaukee Public
Museum
800 W. Wells St.
Milwaukee, WI
53233
(414) 278-2702

The Museum
of Natural History
University of
Wisconsin
900 Reserve St.
Stevens Point, WI
54481
(715) 346-2858

## Wyoming

The Geological
Museum
University
of Wyoming
Laramie, WY 82071
(307) 766-4218

# Art Museums

## Alabama

Birmingham
Museum of Art
2000 8th Ave. N.
Birmingham, AL
35203
(205) 254-2565

The Fine Arts
Museum
of the South
at Mobile
Museum Drive,
Langan Park
Mobile, AL 36689
(205) 343-2667

Montgomery
Museum
of Fine Arts
One Museum Dr.
Montgomery, AL
36123
(205) 244-5700

## Alaska

Alaska State
Museum
395 Whittier
Juneau, AK 99808
(907) 465-2901

Anchorage
Museum
of History and Art
121 W. Seventh Ave.
Anchorage, AK
99501
(907) 343-4326

## Arizona

Northern Arizona
University
Art Gallery
Flagstaff, AZ
(602) 523-3471

Phoenix
Art Museum
1625 N. Central Ave.
Phoenix, AZ 85004
(602) 257-1880

Scottsdale Center
for the Arts
7383 Scottsdale Mall
Scottsdale, AZ 85251
(602) 994-2301

Tempe Arts Center
54 West First St.
Tempe, AZ 85281
(602) 968-0888

Tucson
Museum of Art
140 N. Main Ave.
Tucson, AZ 85701
(602) 624-2333

Yuma Fine Arts
Association
281 Gila St.
Yuma, AZ 85364
(602) 783-2314

## Arkansas

The Arkansas
Arts Center
MacArthur Park
Little Rock, AR
72203
(501) 372-4000

Fort Smith
Art Center
423 N. 6th St.
Fort Smith, AR
72901
(501) 782-6371

The University
Museum
University
of Arkansas
Fayetteville, AR
72701
(501) 575-3555

## California

**Asian Art Museum
of San Francisco**
Golden Gate Park
San Francisco, CA
94118
(415) 668-8922

**Crocker
Art Museum**
216 O St.
Sacramento, CA
95814
(916) 449-5423

**Cunningham
Memorial
Art Gallery**
1930 R St.
Bakersfield, CA
93303
(805) 323-7219

**The Fine Arts
Museums
of San Francisco**
Lincoln Park
San Francisco, CA
94121
(415) 750-3600

**Fowler Museum
of Cultural History**
University
of California
Los Angeles, CA
90024
(213) 825-4361

**Fresno Art Museum**
2233 N. First St.
Fresno, CA 93703
(209) 485-4810

**Fresno
Metropolitan
Museum**
1555 Van Ness Ave.
Fresno, CA 93721
(209) 441-1444

**J. Paul Getty
Museum**
17985 Pacific Coast
Highway
Malibu, CA 90265
(213) 459-7611

**LaJolla Museum
of Contemporary
Art**
700 Prospect St.
LaJolla, CA 92037
(619) 454-3541

**Los Angeles
County Museum**
5905 Wilshire Blvd.
Los Angeles, CA
90036
(213) 857-6111

**The Museum
of African
American Art**
4005 Crenshaw
Blvd., 3rd Fl.
Los Angeles, CA
90008
(213) 294-7071

**Newport Harbor
Art Museum**
850 San Clemente
Dr.
Newport Beach, CA
92660
(714) 759-1122

**The Oakland
Museum**
1000 Oak St.
Oakland, CA 94607
(415) 273-3401

**Pacific Asia
Museum**
46 N. Los Robles Ave.
Pasadena, CA
91101
(818) 449-2742

**Palm Springs
Desert Museum**
101 Museum Drive
Palm Springs, CA
92262
(619) 325-7186

**Plaza De La Raza,
Inc.**
3541 N. Mission Rd.
Los Angeles, CA
90031
(213) 223-2475

**Redding Museum
and Art Center**
56 Quartz Hill Rd.
Redding, CA 96003
(916) 225-4155

San Diego
Museum of Art,
Balboa Park
San Diego, CA
92101
(619) 232-7931

San Francisco
Museum
of Modern Art
401 Van Ness Ave.
San Francisco, CA
94102
(415) 863-8800

San Jose
Museum of Art
110 S. Market St.
San Jose, CA 95113
(408) 294-2787

University Art
Museum
2626 Bancroft Way
Berkeley, CA 94720
(415) 642-1207

# Colorado

The Aspen Art
Museum
590 N. Mill St.
Aspen, CO 81611
(303) 925-8050

Colorado Springs
Fine Arts Center
30 W. Dale St.
Colorado Springs,
CO 80903
(719) 634-5581

The Denver Art
Museum
100 W. 14th Ave.
Parkway
Denver, CO 80204
(303) 575-2295

Sangre de Christo
Arts Center
210 N. Santa Fe Ave.
Pueblo, CO 81003
(719) 543-0130

University
of Colorado
Museum
Broadway, between
15th & 16th Sts.
Boulder, CO 80309
(719) 492-6165

# Connecticut

Davison Art Center
Wesleyan University
301 High St.
Middletown, CT
06457
(203) 347-9411

Hill-Stead Museum
35 Mountain Rd.
Farmington, CT
06032
(203) 677-4787

Museum
of Art, Science
and Industry
4450 Park Ave.
Bridgeport, CT
06604
(203) 372-3521

New Britain
Museum
of American Art
56 Lexington St.
New Britain, CT
06052
(203) 229-0257

Wadsworth
Atheneum
600 Main St.
Hartford, CT 06103
(203) 278-2670

Whitney Museum
of American Arts
One Champion
Plaza
Stamford, CT 06921
(203) 358-7652

Yale University
Art Gallery
1111 Chapel St.
New Haven, CT
06520
(203) 432-0600

# Delaware

Delaware
Art Museum
2301 Kentmere Pkwy.
Wilmington, DE
19806
(302) 571-9590

# District of Columbia

**The Corcoran Gallery of Art**
17 St. & New York Ave., NW
Washington, DC 20006
(202) 638-3211

**Dumbarton Oaks House, Library & Collection**
2715 Q St. NW
Washington, DC 20007
(202) 342-3200

**Howard University Gallery of Art**
2455 6th St., NW
Washington, DC 20059
(202) 636-7047

**Meridian House International**
1630 Crescent Pl., NW
Washington, DC 20009
(202) 667-6800

**Museum of Modern Art of Latin America**
201 18th St., NW
Washington, DC 20006
(202) 789-6019

**National Gallery of Art**
4th St. & Constitution Ave, NW
Washington, DC 20565
(202) 737-4215

**National Museum of Women in the Arts**
1250 New York Ave., NW
Washington, DC 20005
(202) 783-5000

**The Octagon**
1799 New York Ave., NW
Washington, DC 20006
(202) 638-3105

**The Phillips Collection**
1600 21st St. NW
Washington, DC 20009
(202) 387-2151

**Smithsonian Institution**
(collection of history, science, art, and air/space museums)
1000 Jefferson Dr.
Washington, DC 20560
(202) 357-1300

**The White House**
1600 Pennsylvania Ave., NW
Washington, DC 20500
(202) 456-1414

# Florida

**Boca Raton Museum of Art**
801 W. Palmetto Park Rd.
Boca Raton, FL 33486
(407) 392-2500

**Center for the Fine Arts**
101 W. Flagler St.
Miami, FL 33130
(305) 375-1700

**Cummer Gallery of Art**
829 Riverside Ave.
Jacksonville, FL 32204

**Jacksonville Art Museum**
4160 Boulevard Center Dr.
Jacksonville, FL 32207
(904) 398-8336

Lowe Art Museum
University
of Miami
1301 Stanford Dr.
Coral Gables, FL
33146
(305) 284-3535

The Morikami
Museum
of Japanese
Culture
4000 Morikami
Park Rd.
Delray Beach, FL
33446
(407) 499-0631

Museum of Art
1 E. Las Olas Blvd.
Fort Lauderdale, FL
33301
(305) 525-5500

Museum of Arts
and Sciences
1040 Museum Blvd.
Daytona Beach, FL
32014
(904) 255-0285

Museum
of Fine Arts
255 Beach Dr., NE
St. Petersburg, FL
33701
(813) 896-2667

Norton Gallery
of Art
1451 S. Olive Ave.
West Palm Beach,
FL 33401
(407) 832-5194

Orlando Museum
of Art
2416 North Mills
Ave.
Orlando, FL 32803
(305) 896-4231

Pensacola Museum
of Art
407 S. Jefferson St.
Pensacola, FL 32501
(904) 432-6247

Tampa Museum
of Art
601 Doyle Carlton
Dr.
Tampa, FL 33602
(813) 223-8130

## Georgia

The Columbus
Museum
1251 Wynnton Rd.
Columbus, GA
31906
(404) 322-0400

Georgia Museum
of Art
The University
of Georgia
Jackson St.
Athens, GA 30602
(404) 542-3255

The High Museum
of Art
1280 Peachtree St.,
NE
Atlanta, GA 30309
(404) 892-3600

Museum of Arts
and Sciences
4182 Forsyth Rd.
Macon, GA 31210
(912) 477-3232

Telfair Academy
of Arts
and Sciences
121 Bernard St.
Savannah, GA
31401
(912) 232-1177

## Hawaii

Bishop Museum
1525 Bernice St.
Honolulu, HI 96766
(808) 847-3511

Honolulu Academy
of Arts
900 S. Beretania St.
Honolulu, HI 96814
(808) 538-3693

Kauai Museum
4428 Rice St.
Lihue, HI 96766
(808) 245-6931

## Idaho

**Boise Art Museum**
670 S. Julia Davis Dr.
Boise, ID 83702
(208) 345-8330

## Illinois

**Art Institute
of Chicago**
Michigan Ave.
& Adams St.
Chicago, IL 60603
(312) 443-3600

**Augustana College
Gallery of Art**
7th Ave. & 38th St.
Rock Island, IL
61201
(309) 794-7469

**Chicago
Architecture
Foundation**
1800 S. Prairie Ave.
Chicago, IL 60616
(312) 326-1393

Illinois
**State Museum**
Spring & Edwards Sts.
Springfield, IL
62706
(217) 782-7386

**Krannert
Art Museum**
University of Illinois
500 E. Peabody St.
Champaign, IL
61820

Lakeview Museum
of Arts
and Sciences
1125 West Lake Ave.
Peoria, IL 61614
(309) 686-7000

**Museum
of Contemporary
Art**
237 E. Ontario St.
Chicago, IL 60611
(312) 280-2660

**Oriental Institute
Museum**
University
of Chicago
1155 E. 58th St.
Chicago, IL 60637
(312) 702-9520

**Quincy Art Center**
1515 Jersey St.
Quincy, IL 62301
(217) 223-5900

**Quincy Museum
of Natural History
and Art**
1601 Maine St.
Quincy, IL 62301
(217) 224-7669

**Rockford Art
Museum**
711 N. Main St.
Rockford, IL 61103
(815) 965-3131

University Museum
Southern Illinois
University
Carbondale, IL
62901
(618) 453-5388

Frank Lloyd
Wright Home
and Studio
951 Chicago Ave.
Oak Park IL 60302
(708) 848-1976

## Indiana

**Ball State
University
Art Gallery**
200 University Ave.
Muncie, IN 47306
(317) 285-5242

**Eiteljorg Museum
of American
Indian
and Western Art**
500 W. Washington
Indianapolis, IN
46204
(317) 636-9378

**Evansville Museum
of Arts & Science**
411 SE Reverside Dr.
Evansville, IN 47713
(812) 425-2406

Fort Wayne
Museum of Art
311 E. Main St.
Fort Wayne, IN
46802
(219) 422-6467

Greater Lafayette
Museum of Art
101 S. Ninth St.
Lafayette, IN 47901
(317) 742-1128

Indiana University
Art Museum
Indiana University
Bloomington, IL
47405
(812) 855-5445

Indianapolis
Museum
of Art
1200 W. 38th St.
Indianapolis, IN
46208
(317) 923-1331

Midwest Museum
of American Art
429 Main St.
Elkhart, IN 46515
(219) 293-6660

The Snite Museum
of Art
University
of Notre Dame
Notre Dame, IN
46556
(219) 239-5466

South Bend
Art Center
120 S. Joseph St.
South Bend, IN
46601
(219) 284-9102

Sheldon Swope
Art Museum
25 S. 7th St.
Terra Haute, IN
47807
(812) 238-1676

## Iowa

Brunnier Gallery
and Museum
Scheman Building
Iowa State
University
Ames, IA 50011
(515) 294-3342

Cedar Rapids
Museum of Art
410 Third Ave. SE
Cedar Rapids, IA
52401
(319) 366-7503

Davenport
Museum of Art
1737 W. Twelfth St.
Davenport, IA
52804
(319) 326-7804

Des Moines
Art Center
4700 Grand Ave.
Des Moines, IA
50319
(515) 277-4405

Dubuque Museum
of Art
8th & Central
Dubuque, IA 52001
(319) 557-1851

Gallery of Art
University
of Northern Iowa
Art Building
Cedar Falls, IA
50614
(319) 273-2077

University of Iowa
Museum of Art
North Riverside Dr.
Iowa City, IA 52242
(319) 335-1727

Winterset Art
Center
508 E. Jeff St.
Winterset, IA 50273
(515) 462-3741

## Kansas

Mulvane Art
Museum
17th & Jewell
Topeka, KS 66621
(913) 295-6324

Spencer Museum
of Art
University of Kansas
1301 Mississippi St.
Lawrence, KS 66045
(913) 864-4710

The Wichita
Art Association
9112 E. Central
Wichita, KS 67206
(316) 686-6687

Wichita
Art Museum
619 Stackman Dr.
Wichita, KS 67203
(316) 268-4921

**Kentucky**

Behringer-
Crawford Museum
1600 Montague Rd.
Devou Park
Covington, KY
41012
(606) 491-4003

Owensboro
Museum
of Fine Art
901 Frederica St.
Owensboro, KY
42301
(502) 685-3181

J.B. Speed
Art Museum
2035 S. Third St.
Louisville, KY 40208
(502) 636-2893

The Kentucky
Museum
Western Kentucky
University
Bowling Green, KY
42101
(502) 745-2592

University
of Kentucky
Art Museum
Rose and Euclid
Lexington, KY
40506
(606) 257-5716

**Louisiana**

Alexandria
Museum of Art
933 Main St.
Alexandria, LA
71301
(318) 443-3458

Louisiana Arts
and Science Center
100 S. River Rd.
Baton Rouge, LA
70801
(504) 344-9463

Masur Museum
of Art
1400 S. Grand
Monroe, LA 71457
(318) 329-2237

Meadows Museum
of Art
Centenary College
2911 Centenary
Blvd.
Shreveport, LA
71104
(318) 869-5169

New Orleans
Museum of Art
City Park
New Orleans, LA
70119
(504) 488-2631

The R.W. Norton
Art Gallery
4747 Creswell Ave.
Shreveport, LA
71106
(318) 865-4201

**Maine**

Bowdoin College
Museum of Art
Walker Art Buidling
Brunswick, ME
04011
(207) 725-3275

Museum of Art
of Ogunquit
Shore Rd.
Ogunquit, ME
03907
(207) 646-4909

Portland Museum
of Art
Seven Congress
Square
Portland, ME 04101
(207) 775-6148

## Maryland

Academy
of the Arts
106 South St.
Easton, MD 21601
(301) 822-0455

The Baltimore
Museum of Art
Art Museum Drive
Baltimore, MD
21218
(301) 396-7101

Maryland Museum
of African Art
5434 Vantage Point
Columbia, MD
21044
(301) 730-2621

Walters Art Gallery
600 N. Charles St.
Baltimore, MD
21201
(301) 547-9000

## Massachusetts

The Berkshire
Museum
39 South St.
Pittsfield, MA 01201
(413) 443-7171

Fuller Museum
of Art
455 Oak St.
Brockton, MA 02401
(508) 588-6000

The Institute
of Contemporary
Art
955 Boylston St.
Boston, MA 02115
(617) 266-5151

Museum
of Fine Arts
465 Huntington Ave.
Boston, MA 02115
(617) 267-9300

Provincetown
Art Museum
460 Commercial St.
Provincetown, MA
02657
(617) 487-1750

Norman Rockwell
Museum
Main St.
Stockbridge, MA
01262
(413) 298-3944

Arthur M. Sackler
Museum
485 Broadway
Cambridge, MA
02138
(617) 495-9400

Worchester Art
Museum
55 Salisbury Rd.
Worchester, MA
01609
(508) 799-4406

## Michigan

Art Center
of Battle Creek
265 E. Emmett St.
Battle Creek, MI
49017
(616) 962-9511

Jesse Besser
Museum
491 Johnson St.
Alpena, MI 49707
(517) 356-2202

Cranbrook
Academy
of Art Museum,
Cranbrook
Institute of Science
500 Lone Pine Rd.
Bloomfield Hills, MI
48013
(313) 645-3323

Detroit Institute
of Arts
5200 Woodward
Ave.
Detroit, MI 48202
(313) 833-7900

Flint Institute
of Arts
1120 E. Kearsley St.
Flint, MI 48503
(313) 234-1695

Grand Rapids
Art Museum
155 N. Division
Grand Rapids, MI
49503
(616) 459-4677

Kalamazoo
Institute of Arts
314 S. Park St.
Kalamazoo, MI
49007
(616) 349-7775

Kresge Art Museum
Michigan State
University
East Lansing, MI
48824
(517) 355-7631

Midland Arts
Council,
Midland Center
for the Arts
1801 W. St. Andrews
Midland, MI 48640
(517) 631-3250

Museum of Arts
and History
1115 Sixth St.
Port Huron, MI
48060
(313) 982-0891

Muskegon
Museum of Art
296 W. Webster
Muskegon, MI
49440
(616) 722-2600

Public Museum
of Grand Rapids
54 Jefferson S.E.
Grand Rapids, MI
49503
(616) 456-3977

Saginaw
Art Museum
1126 N. Michigan
Ave.
Saginaw, MI 48602
(517) 754-2491

University
of Michigan
Museum of Art
525 S. State St.
Ann Arbor, MI
48109
(313) 764-0395

## Minnesota

Minneapolis
Institute of Arts
2400 Third Ave. So.
Minneapolis, MN
55404
(612) 870-3000

Minnesota
Museum of Art
Fifth & Market
St. Paul, MN 55102
(612) 292-4355

Plains Art Museum
521 Main Ave.
Moorhead, MN
56560
(218) 236-7171

Tweed Museum
of Art
University of
Minnesota
Duluth, MN 55812
(218) 726-8222

Walker Art Center
Vineland Place
Minneapolis, MN
55403
(612) 375-7600

## Mississippi

Mississippi
Museum of Art
201 E. Pascagoula St.
Jackson, MS 39201
(601) 960-1515

Mississippi
Museum
of Art/Gulf Coast
136 George E. Ohr St.
Biloxi, MS 39530
(601) 374-5547

Lauren Rogers
Museum of Art
5th Ave. at 7th St.
Laurel, MS 39440
(601) 649-6374

University
Museums
The University
of Mississippi
University, MS
38677
(601) 232-7073

## Missouri

Albrecht Art
Museum
2818 Frederick Blvd.
St. Joseph, MO
64506
(816) 233-7003

Museum
of Art and
Archaeology
University
of Missouri
Columbia, MO
65211
(314) 882-3591

The Nelson-Atkins
Museum of Art
4525 Oak St.
Kansas City, MO
64111
(816) 561-4000

St. Louis
Art Museum
Forest Park
St. Louis, MO 63110
(314) 721-0067

Springfield
Art Mueum
1111 E. Brookside Dr.
Springfield, MO
65807
(417) 866-2716

Missoula Museum
of the Arts
335 N. Pattee
Missoula, MT
59802
(406) 728-0447

C.M. Russell
Museum
400 13th St. North
Great Falls, MT
59401
(406) 727-8787

Yellowstone
Art Center
401 N. 27th St.
Billings, MT 59101
(406) 256-6804

## Montana

Butte-Silver Bow
Arts Chateau
321 W. Broadway
Butte, MT 59701
(406) 723-7600

Hockaday Center
for the Arts
Second Ave. E. &
Third St.
Kalispell, MT 59901
(406) 755-5268

## Nebraska

Joslyn Art Museum
2200 Dodge St.
Omaha, NE 68102
(402) 342-3300

Museum
of Nebraska Art
24th & Central
Kearney, NE 68848
(308) 234-8559

Sheldon Memorial
Art Gallery
12th & R Sts.
Lincoln, NE 68588
(402) 472-2461

## Nevada

Las Vegas
Art Museum
3333 W. Washington
Las Vegas, NV
89107
(702) 647-4300

Nevada Museum
of Art
160 W. Liberty
Reno, NV 89501
(702) 329-3333

# New Hampshire

The Currier
Gallery of Art
192 Orange St.
Manchester, NH
03104
(603) 669-6144

University
Art Galleries
University of New
Hampshire
Durham, NH 03824
(603) 862-3712

# New Jersey

African Art
Museum
of the S.M.A.
Fathers
23 Bliss Ave.
Tenafly, NJ 07670
(201) 567-0450

The Art Museum
Princeton Univesity
Princeton, NJ 08544
(609) 452-3788

Bergen Museum
of Art & Science
Ridgewood
& Farview Aves.
Paramus, NJ 07652
(201) 265-1248

Hunterdon
Art Center
7 Center St.
Clinton, NJ 08809
(201) 735-8415

Montclair
Art Museum
3 South Mountain
Ave.
Montclair, NJ 07042
(201) 746-5555

Jane Voorhees
Zimmerli
Art Museum
Rutgers University
New Brunswick, NJ
08903
(201) 932-7237

# New Mexico

Institute
of American Indian
Arts Museum
1369 Cerrillos Rd.
Santa Fe, NM 87504
(505) 988-6281

Museum
of Fine Arts
107 W. Palace
Santa Fe, NM 87501
(505) 827-4468

Museum
of New Mexico
113 Lincoln Ave.
Santa Fe, NM 87504
(502) 827-6450

Roswell Museum
and Art Center
100 West 11th
Roswell, NM 88201
(505) 624-6744

University
Art Museum
The University
of New Mexico
Albuquerque, NM
87131
(505) 277-4001

# New York

(Note: New York
City has a separate
section)

Albany Institute
of History & Art
125 Washington
Ave.
Albany, NY 12210
(518) 463-4478

Albright-Knox
Art Gallery
1285 Elmwood Ave.
Buffalo, NY 14222
(716) 882-1958

Arnot Art Museum
235 Lake St.
Elmira, NY 14901
(607) 734-3697

The Corning
Museum of Glass
1 Museum Way
Corning, NY 14830
(607) 937-5371

Everson Museum
of Art of Syracuse
and Onondaga
County
401 Harrison St.
Syracuse, NY 13202
(315) 474-6064

Fine Art Museum
of Long Island
295 Fulton Ave.
Hempstead, NY
11550
(516) 481-5700

The Hyde
Collection
161 Warren St.
Glen Falls, NY
12801
(518) 792-1761

International
Museum
of Photography
George Eastman
House
900 East Ave.
Rochester, NY 14607
(716) 271-3361

Herbert F. Johnson
Museum of Art
Cornell University
Ithaca, NY 14853
(607) 255-6464

Munson-Williams-
Proctor Institute
Museum of Art
310 Genesee St.
Utica, NY 13502
(315) 797-0000

The Parrish
Art Museum
25 Job's Lane
Southampton, NY
11968
(516) 283-2118

Roberson Center
for the Arts
and Sciences
30 Front St.
Binghamton, NY
13905
(607) 772-0660

Schnectady
Museum
and Planetarium
Nott Terrace Heights
Schenectady, NY
12308
(518) 382-7890

Schweinfurth
Memorial
Art Center
205 Genesee St.
Auburn, NY 13021
(315) 255-1553

Staten Island
Institute
of Arts
and Sciences
75 Stuyvesant Place
Staten Island, NY
10301
(718) 727-1135

# New York City

The Center
for African Art
54 East 68th St.
New York, NY 11201
(212) 861-1200

The Cloisters
190 3rd St. -
Fort Tryon Park
New York, NY 10040
(212) 923-3700

Cooper-Hewitt
Museum,
The Smithsonian
Institution
Museum of Design
2 East 91st St.
New York, NY 10128
(212) 860-6868

El Museo del Barrio
1230 Fifth Ave.
New York, NY 10029
(212) 831-7272

The Frick
Collection
1 East 70th St.
New York, NY 10021
(212) 288-0700

Solomon R.
Guggenheim
Museum
1071 Fifth Ave.
New York, NY 10128
(212) 360-3500

The Metropolitan
Museum of Art
Fifth Ave. at 82nd St.
New York, NY 10028
(212) 879-5500

Museum
of American
Folk Art
Two Lincoln Square
New York, NY 10023
(212) 977-7170

The Museum
of Modern Art
11 W. 53rd St.
New York, NY 10019
(212) 708-9400

The New Museum
of Contemporary
Art
583 Broadway
New York, NY 10012
(212) 219-1222

The Studio
Museum in Harlem
144 W. 125th St.
New York, NY 10027
(212) 864-4500

Whitney Museum
of American Art
945 Madison Ave.
New York, NY 10021
(212) 570-3600

# North
# Carolina

Asheville
Art Museum
Asheville Civic
Center
Asheville, NC 28801
(704) 253-3227

Fayetteville
Museum of Art
839 Stamper Rd.
Fayetteville, NC
28301
(919) 323-1776

Greenville
Museum of Art
802 Evans St.
Greenville, NC
27834
(919) 758-1946

Mint Museum
of Art
2730 Randolph Rd.
Charlotte, NC
28207
(704) 337-2000

Museum of Early
Southern
Decorative Arts
924 S. Main St.
Winston-Salem, NC
27101
(919) 721-7360

North Carolina
Museum of Art
2110 Blue Ridge
Blvd.
Raleigh, NC 27607
(919) 833-1935

# North
# Dakota

Art Gallery
North Dakota
State University
Fargo, ND 58105
(701) 237-8236

North Dakota
Museum of Art
University
of North Dakota
Grand Forks, ND
58202
(701) 777-3650

# Ohio

Allen Memorial
Art Museum
Oberlin College
Oberlin, OH 44074
(216) 775-8665

Akron Art Museum
70 E. Market St.
Akron, OH 44308
(216) 376-9185

The Butler Institute
of American Art
524 Wick Ave.
Youngstown, OH
44502
(216) 743-1711

The Canton
Art Institute
1001 Market Ave. N.
Canton, OH 44702
(216) 453-7666

Cincinnati
Art Musem
Eden Park
Cincinnati, OH
45202
(513) 721-5204

The Cleveland
Museum of Art
11150 East Blvd.
Cleveland, OH
44106
(216) 421-7340

Columbus
Museum of Art
480 E. Broad St.
Columbus, OH
43215
(614) 221-6801

The Contemporary
Arts Center
115 E. 5th St.
Cincinnati, OH
45202
(513) 721-0390

Dayton
Art Institute
Forest & Riverview
Aves.
Dayton, OH 45405
(513) 223-5277

The Toledo
Museum of Art
2445 Monroe St.
Toledo, OH 43620
(419) 225-8000

## Oklahoma

Charles B. Goddard
Center for Visual
and Performing
Arts
First Ave. & D St SW
Ardmore, OK 73401
(405) 226-0909

Oklahoma City
Art Museum
3113 Pershing Blvd.
Oklahoma City OK
73107
(405) 946-4477

Oklahoma
Museum of Art
7316 Nichols Rd.
Oklahoma City, OK
73120
(405) 840-2759

Philbrook
Museum of Art
2727 S. Rockford Rd.
Tulsa, OK 74114

## Oregon

Portland
Art Museum
1219 SW Park Ave.
Portland, OR 97205
(503) 226-2811

University
of Oregon
Museum of Art
1430 Johnson Lane
Eugene, OR 97403
(503) 686-3027

## Pennsylvania

Allentown
Art Museum
Fifth & Court Sts.
Allentown, PA
18105
(215) 432-4333

The Carnegie
Museum of Art
440 Forbes Ave.
Pittsburgh, PA
15213
(412) 622-3200

Erie Art Museum
411 State St.
Erie, PA 16501
(814) 459-5477

Philadelphia
Museum of Art
26th St. and the
Parkway
Philadelphia, PA
19130
(215) 763-8100

Westmoreland
Museum of Art
221 N. Main St.
Greensburg, PA
15601
(412) 837-1500

## Rhode Island

Newport
Art Museum
76 Bellevue Ave.
Newport, RI 02840
(401) 847-0179

Museum of Art
Rhode Island School
of Design
224 Benefit St.
Providence, RI
02903
(401) 331-3511

## South Carolina

Columbia
Museum of Art
1112 Bull St.
Columbia, SC
29201
(803) 799-2810

Gibbes
Museum of Art
135 Meeting St.
Charleston, SC
29401
(803) 722-2706

## South Dakota

Civic Fine Arts
Center
235 W. Tenth St.
Sioux Falls, SD
57102
(605) 336-1167

Dahl Fine Arts
Center
713 Seventh St.
Rapid City, SD
57701
(605) 394-4101

Sioux Indian
Museum
and Crafts Center
515 West Blvd.
Rapid City, SD
57701
(605) 348-0557

South Dakota
Art Museum
Medary Ave. at
Dunn St.
Brookings, SD
57007
(605) 688-5423

University
Art Galleries
Warren M. Lee
Center
University of South
Dakota
Vermillion, SD
57069
(605) 677-5636

## Tennessee

Country Music
Hall of Fame
and Museum
4 Music Square East
Nashville, TN 37263
(615) 256-1639

The Dixon Gallery
and Gardens
4339 Park Ave.
Memphis, TN 38117
(901) 761-5250

Hunter
Museum of Art
10 Bluff View
Chattanooga, TN
37403
(615) 267-0968

Knoxville
Museum of Art
1010 Laurel Ave.
Knoxville, TN
37916
(615) 525-6101

Memphis Brooks
Museum of Art
Overton Park
Memphis, TN 38112
(901) 722-3525

Nashville
Parthenon
Centennial Park
Nashville, TN 37203
(615) 259-6358

# Texas

**Abilene Fine Arts
Museum**
801 S. Mockingbird
Abilene, TX 79605
(915) 673-4587

**Amarillo
Art Center**
2200 S. Van Buren
Amarillo, TX 79109
(806) 371-5050

**Archer Huntington
Art Gallery**
University of Texas,
Austin
23rd
& San Jacinto Sts.
Austin, TX 78712
(512) 471-7324

**Art Museum
of Southeast Texas**
500 Main St.
Beaumont, TX
77704
(409) 832-3432

**Contemporary Arts
Museum**
5216 Montrose
Houston, TX 77006
(713) 526-0773

**Dallas
Museum of Art**
1717 N. Harwood
Dallas, TX 75201
(214) 922-0220

**El Paso
Museum of Art**
1211 Montana Ave.
El Paso, TX 79902
(915) 541-4040

**Kimbell
Art Museum**
3333 Camp Bowie
Blvd.
Fort Worth, TX
76107
(817) 332-8451

**Laguna Gloria
Art Museum**
3809 W. 35th St.
Austin, TX 78731
(512) 458-8191

**Museum of Fine
Arts of Houston**
1001 Bissonnet
Houston, TX 77005
(713) 526-1361

**Marion Koogler
McNay
Art Museum**
6000 N. New
Braunfels Ave.
San Antonio, TX
78209
(512) 824-5368

**San Antonio
Museum of Art**
200 West Jones Ave.
San Antonio, TX
78299
(512) 226-5544

**Tyler
Museum of Art**
1300 S. Mahon Ave.
Tyler, TX 75701
(214) 595-1001

**Wichita Falls
Museum
and Art Center**
2 Eureka Circle
Wichita Falls, TX
76308
(817) 692-0923

# Utah

**Utah Museum
of Fine Arts**
University of Utah
Salt Lake City, UT
84112
(801) 581-7332

**Brigham Young
University Museum
of Fine Arts**
Harris Fine Arts
Center
Provo, UT 84602
(801) 378-2818

# Vermont

**The Bennington
Museum**
W. Main St.
Bennington, VT
05201
(802) 447-1571

The Sheldon
Art Museum
1 Park St.
Middlebury, VT
05753
(802) 388-2117

# Virginia

Bayly Art Museum
Univerity
of Virginia
Charlottesville, VA
22903
(804) 924-3592

The Chrysler
Museum
Olney Rd. &
Mowbray Arch
Norfolk, VA 23510
(804) 622-1211

Hampton
University
Museum
Hampton
University
Hampton, VA
23668
(804) 727-5308

Maier
Museum of Art
Quinlan St.
Lynchburg, VA
24503
(804) 846-9696

Roanoke Museum
of Fine Arts
One Market Square
Roanoke, VA 24011
(703) 342-5760

Virginia Beach
Center for the Arts
2200 Park Ave.
Virginia Beach, VA
23451
(804) 425-0000

Virginia Museum
of Fine Arts
2800 Grove Ave.
Richmond, VA
23221
(804) 367-0844

# Washington

Bellevue
Art Museum
301 Bellevue Square
Bellevue, WA 98004
(206) 454-3322

Larson Museum
and Gallery
S. 16th Ave. & Nob
Hill Blvd.
Yakima, WA 98907
(509) 575-2402

Maryhill
Museum of Art
35 Maryhill
Museum Dr.
Goldendale, WA
98620
(509) 773-3733

Museum of Art
Washington State
University
Pullman, WA 99164
(509) 335-1910

Seattle
Art Museum
100 University St.
Seattle, WA 98101
(206) 625-8900

Tacoma
Art Museum
12th & Pacific Ave.
Tacoma, WA 98402
(206) 272-4258

Whatcom Museum
of History and Art
121 Prospect St.
Bellingham, WA
98225
(206) 676-6981

Wing Luke
Asian Museum
407 Seventh Ave. So.
Seattle, WA 98104
(206) 623-5124

# West Virginia

Huntington
Museum of Art
2033 McCoy Rd.
Huntington, WV
25701
(304) 529-2701

Parkersburg
Art Center
220 Eight St.
Parkersburg, WV
26101
(304) 485-3859

## Wisconsin

Elvehjem
Museum of Art
800 University Ave.
Madison, WI 53706
(608) 263-2246

John Michael
Kohler Arts Center
608 New York Ave.
Sheboygan, WI
53081
(414) 458-6144

Madison
Art Center
211 State St.
Madison, WI 53703
(608) 257-0158

Milwaukee
Art Museum
750 N. Lincoln
Memorial Dr.
Milwaukee, WI
53202
(414) 271-9508

Milwaukee
Public Museum
800 W. Wells St.
Milwaukee, WI
53233
(414) 278-2702

Ozaukee
Art Center
W 62 N 718
Riveredge Dr.
Cedarburg, WI
53012
(414) 377-8230

Paine Art Center
and Arboretum
1410 Algoma Blvd.
Oshkosh, WI 54901
(414) 235-4530

## Wyoming

Nicolaysen
Art Museum
596 N. Poplar
Casper, WY 82601
(307) 235-5247

University
of Wyoming
Art Museum
Fine Arts Building
Laramie, WY 82071
(307) 766-6622

# Notes on Additional Museums

## About the Author

**Alan R. Gartenhaus** has worked in the field of museum education since 1974. During that time, he served as Education Specialist for the Smithsonian Institution in Washington, D.C., and as Education Curator for the New Orleans Museum of Art. In 1988, he was awarded an Alden B. Dow Fellowship for his work involving the relationship between museums and creative thinking.

Currently, Mr. Gartenhaus is the publishing editor of *The Docent Educator*, a journal for those who teach in museums, zoos, and parks. In addition, he writes, teaches, and conducts seminars and workshops for museums, universities, and school systems around the country. Mr. Gartenhaus lives in Seattle, Washington and Kamuela, Hawaii.

# Notes

# **Notes**

# Notes

# Notes

# Notes